PARIS TO WASHINGTON:

MY DESTINY

MRVO

ISBN: 978-1-950652-04-4 (Paperback)
ISBN: 978-1-950652-01-3 (Hardcover)

A YOUNG LADY, THE ELDEST of ten, sat on a train from Paris to Mulhouse. She thought, *Why am I on this train!* Life was not easy. Her mother was pregnant with her tenth child, her father was killed in an accident, probably by a machine used on the land, mother never mentioned anything about it, the facts were the family was fatherless and there she was, having the responsibility of raising her siblings.

Mittelwhir, a village where Mother was born on the 15th of August 1910 in the southern part of Alsace, near Colmar, consisted mainly of the Wurtz family, cousins, and great-cousins. Grandmother married a distant cousin and had ten children — eight girls and two boys. I never met my uncle Emile; he never came back from the war, World War II. Alsace had been a region taken by Germans and retaken by French. One cousin was shot by his other cousin, one being enrolled in the French Army and the other in the German one. This was a very familiar drama for the region. Bang — one was gone.

The three eldest, Louise (my mother), Emilie, and Marguerite tried to find some work. They had ended their last school year and helped with chores. They read all kinds of books (art, music, culture), had a general knowledge of a good education for their time, and they understood German (their second language). They searched ads to find work and decided on three of them. Mother corresponded with a duke in Paris; Emilie with Mr. Schneller, a painter in St-Die, a picturesque town near Switzerland; and Marguerite with another wealthy family in Paris. They were hired to be companions (*dame de compagnie*), play cards, have lunch, go to the theater, and always have a listening ear! Mother never spoke too much about it, though I have a photo of the duke with Mother and me. Their lives would be changed forever — destiny . . .

Mother and Tata (Marguerite) commuted home from work on holidays and some weekends. Mother was taking the train one day, heading home, when she met a handsome man with reddish-blond hair and greenish eyes. He was funny, a gentleman. She laughed and laughed, talked about everything and nothing, and had the time of her life. She was demure, shy, beautiful with dark almost black eyes, and sharp features; she was the best looking of the ten children. He sat next to her on the train. Her trip became the shortest and nicest one she took. He went to his parents' house, she to hers, and they communicated through letters.

My father, Rene, was born on the 25th of April 1914. His oldest brother, Eugene, born on the 25th of September 1907, was in the same situation. After World War I, when they were born, the country was destroyed, the money was sparse, and there were no jobs. Father became a hairstylist — his father's choice — a trade always in need. Eugene became an architect. Before, during, and after the war he had no work. The world was unsettled, so my father took care of his sibling. Later Eugene became part of the group who built the Palais de la Defense. Eugene was a scholar, consumed by books; my father was more of an extravert, an artist, a performer. They both commuted to Alsace whenever they could to be with their parents.

Father had a previous relationship with a young lady in Paris. When Father ended their romance, she took an overdose and died. After months, a year of courtship, Father wed Mother in July 2, 1938, in Paris. They lived in a small apartment on the tenth floor with no elevator. Some windows overlooked adjacent roofs, and they had a skylight. It provided lots of light, and the doves would come and entertain them. Father worked in a hair salon, and Mother as a companion to a duchess. They settled their life together, loving each other, enjoying Paris which had so much to offer. Even if you had a tight budget, you could stroll the streets, discover the architecture, the wonderful parks, fountains, the river Seine with its barges, and the book kiosks along the banks. You could take everything in. Happiness invades your body and your soul; you feel grand, invincible, everything is possible, and you are in love.

Marguerite had met Eugene and wed two years earlier on June 27, 1936, in Paris. They often met with Louise and Rene — two sisters marrying two brothers, quite unusual. They had a lot in common, though different, which made it interesting. Marguerite and Rene were vivacious, always on the go; Louise and Eugene were quiet and listened.

Marguerite and Eugene moved to the 17th arrondissement, Louise and Rene rented an apartment in the 14th, they had different jobs. The foursome saw each other often and went to the theater, opera, and concerts (Eugene and Rene played musical instruments). It was a new world without bounds filled with adventure. The two sisters were great cooks and made wonderful meals pleasing their mates. Their gatherings were joyous and humorous; they were in love and happy. The world was at their feet. Paris embraced them fully.

The world was on fire! It was falling apart. There was unrest everywhere. During the night of November 9, 1938, shops and homes of thousand Jews were trashed as well as synagogues across Germany, Austria, and part of Czechoslovakia; Jews were killed. On September 3, 1939, war was declared on Germany by the United States, Britain, and France. In 1942, the German war machine had rolled over much of Europe. France was occupied, Russia was under attack, and the United States was still gearing up to fight; the Germans seemed unstoppable. Nobody knew what was going to happen. The only communication was the radio. General De Gaulle, head of the resistance from 1940 to 1944, went to London, a safer place. From there he gave instructions to the underground. France was in disarray, and people were scared.

Marguerite had given birth to a daughter named Jacqueline on April 30, 1938, and life became difficult. Eugene was drafted in 1939. After a fierce battle, he found himself the only survivor, his unit destroyed. He made the trip back to Paris from the battlefield on a stolen bicycle. It took him three months going from city to city, town to town, looking for food and water.

Meanwhile, Marguerite and Jacqueline had gone back to her parents in law, to Cernay, where they finally heard from him, and then returned to Paris to join him. Rene helped his brother financially because there were no architecture projects. Then Rene was sent to Germany for forced labor. In the late spring of 1941, Mother was pregnant. Hitler was advancing, occupying Europe, and there was no limit. From Asia to Africa, his goal was to destroy the Jews and anyone who was not Aryan. Millions were sent to concentration camps.

On January 27, 1942, the siren sounded! Planes flew low, and incredible loud noises were followed by many flying machines. Mother was in the middle of contractions;

I was coming into this world! She went down the ten flights of stairs as fast as she could and began walking toward the hospital called "Baudelocque." The loud sirens were a warning that you had to lie flat on the ground and not move. Amidst the sirens, people screamed and ran, not knowing what to do or where to go. We never knew where the bombs were going to strike. Mother's contractions were coming closer. I never knew if she ever made it to the hospital; she never spoke about my birth. But on my birth certificate there was a witness named Lucien Champoux, suggesting I was born in the street.

I came to this world at 3:25 p.m. She named me Monique, a French name, followed by Renee, my father's name. Being the oldest, I was supposed to carry his name. Father was in Germany for forced labor, so Mother was on her own in an occupied country, and here I was. Mother breastfed me, and stood in long lines to get a little food with food stamps. Often there was nothing left, so we made it with what we had. We learned to save and eat whatever was served, in small portions, and be content.

On August the 8, 1943, my sister Annick was born in the same hospital I was supposed to have been born at Baudelocque Hospital named after a midwife, a doctor delivering babies; at that time anything related to health services was a doctor; he was born in 1746 to 1810. However, there were complications. The nurses had to use forceps and accidentally cracked her scull; my sister later would have some epileptic seizures.

All of us had to adjust to the new addition. Mother nurtured my sister because of her problem, and I felt left out. With the unrest in the world — the wars, the occupation — it was very frightening. There were no jobs, people hid (scared), and the country had no direction. There was no leadership, an insecure future, and food was very scarce. My sister had diluted breast milk due to Mother's bad nutrition, and I ended up with lots of water. Sometimes, when we were lucky, I had milk.

One day Mother had enough ingredients to make a cream caramel, a dream treat. As we sat at the table enjoying it, the siren started. There was a loud warning. We had to leave everything in a hurry to go down the ten flights of stairs to the basement. Mother carried my sister while I held on to her skirt, my little legs flying, trying to keep up amid all the people of the building screaming and pushing to get down faster. I can still hear the clicking of the feet on the steps, the humming of the flow of human bodies, and the cry of a child here and there. The orchestrated boot steps from the Germans above us made us shrink, waiting to be discovered. Fear reduces you to nobody, to nothing. It was serious, from babies to the elderly, we all knew it; we all were petrified. My *mouchi* ("handkerchief") was in my hand, right under my nose. It was my safety, my friend. Panic infiltrated the minds of the elderly, the young, and the babies, bringing uncertainty and fear. When the warning was over, we made our way up, climbing the steps. I trailed behind Mother holding to her skirt, afraid to lose her. We made it all right with a sigh of relief on everyone's face. When we arrived to our apartment our treats were gone, to our greatest disappointment. We cried.

One day when we went to the market, a young man walked toward us, and from nowhere a German soldier came, asked him to take his pants down, and then *BANG!* shot him in cold blood. It was horrific for Mother and me. An innocent young man lost his life because he was circumcised. I was two, and I will never forget it. I learned also to know when the German planes were coming, or the Americans, to lie flush with the ground and be still. You very quickly develop a knowledge for survival, even as such a young age. Meanwhile, the war was raging. The Germans though, over too many fronts, started to show fatigue. Thank God Hitler loved Paris and didn't destroy it. One of his goals was to bring all the arts to his country.

It was a turning point in everybody's life. Those who were occupied were stranded with uncertainty, no freedom, scared, and starving. It was hell. Before the war ended, I got bit by a rat and came down with diphtheria. It was when we were in the basement hiding (they were hungry too). I had not been vaccinated. An old doctor living in the building suggested that we move to the country, out of Paris, where they had food and remedies to help me. The duke knew a friend in Luminy, east of Paris, so we packed the few things we had, especially my precious blanket, and we went. I remember the vinegar bath I took to bring my fever down.

We lived in a small, one-level house with an elderly lady, the owner of the place, a friend of the duke, her white hair in a tight chignon, smiling, and very nice. What a change of pace! There were no sirens, no screaming, no running, no airplanes flying over, and no starving. It was a treat and everybody appreciated it. Finally, on May 7, 1945, we got the very big news: THE WAR ENDED. The German Army capitulated without condition thanks to the Americans who came to free us from the German dictatorial and genocide leadership.

It took time for me to recuperate. My sister, now three, was running. We were happy, chasing butterflies, watching birds, and getting the eggs from the chicken coop. It was a new world full of surprises. There was no crisis; it was heaven. I finely got used to it being the three of us when Father came to join us. I had no recollection of him, it was difficult to adjust, it was different. I had to listen to him and obey him. I had two parents now, and I had to comply to my new life very fast. We couldn't stay in Luminy forever. Father had to find a job, so my parents decided to go to Alsace, Cernay, where my father's parents lived. They had a big house, so we packed up and went.

My grandparents had a huge old home. It had three floors, high ceilings, and big windows. It was a corner house made of rough cast cement, very light gray and dark gray shutters, red roof tiles, and a canal running in the back where they used to propel the machines needed for the textile factory. Cernay had been a medieval, fortified city once with some remnants of the rampart still there — the entrance door, the towers, and the water around. The church was built in the center of the town, as well a big fountain, and houses were gathered along the roads. Three factories were in town so people had jobs, especially after the war. Houses

were destroyed, and many needed repaired. Ours had a
split, about a foot, from top to bottom. I remembered my
grandparents and parents using materials to stop the draft in
the winter or the heat in the summer. Regardless of how it
looked we had a home.

Grandfather was a journalist and knew a lot of
influential people. He got into politics. He leaned toward
socialism and was friends with the Russians. He was
inflexible; he was right all the time and it was his way
or no way. He was born and raised when Alsace was
German, from 1871 to 1918; by the Traite of Versailles
Alsace became part of France until the Reich took over
from 1940 to 1944, after fierce battles with the help of
the Americans the French reclaimed it, liberated in1945.
People living in this part of France are different from
any one, they are working hard, honest, loyal, a friend
for ever, neat, and like my grandfather strong minded.
Grandmother lived in his shadow. She never had an
opinion and attended to his needs and desires. As I grew
older I distanced myself from them. I would kiss them
every morning and every night; we had to go through
their quarters to reach the third floor where our bedrooms
were. They spoke German, French, and a dialect
(Alsacien); we only knew French.

When the Germans occupied the town they changed
the names of the streets to German. After World War II
the city, little by little, restored them back to French. In
school they replaced the books and French was again the
official language. Everybody had to register their birth
dates, birth places in order to get their own identities.
Builders put a steel plate around our house to correct the
split, and it was re-cemented; we had a new house.

On August 11, 1946, we were christened at the Lutheran Church in Colmar. The whole Wurst family came by motorcycles, trucks, or any public transportation. It was a happy time getting to know members of my family, exchange thoughts, enjoy life, have freedom, and be content. On June 5, 1947, after coming home from school, I was greeted by a lady in a white uniform asking my sister and me to follow her. She went to my parents' bedroom, which was on the second floor. My mother was in a big bed with all types of pillows around her. She seemed so happy, smiling. I had never seen her so content, so beautiful. Then I discovered a little bed in the corner. I looked in it and there was a baby; the stork brought us a brother! Francis Claude. I was in shock! We didn't need this. We had just adjusted to our new life, and now we had a new addition. I glanced outside, and a ray of sunshine grazed Mother's happy face. It was so comforting, and all the uncertainty washed away. I jumped from one foot to the other, tilting my head from one side to the other, my golden locks flying. The summer was ending, school was starting, and the nuns were our teachers. They were strict but quite good. I didn't have any problems. My early life was nice and easy.

Father was an amazing man. He was always working at the salon or taking care of the vineyard. Grandfather had some land where he grew vine stocks and fruit trees — mirabelles, cherries, plums, quetsches (a smaller kind of plum), blackberries. It was very busy keeping the grounds clear of weeds and harvesting — selecting and putting the fruits in different categories. In the fall we had a stack of wood delivered in front of the house the width of the street. Friends and Father cut the logs with borrowed axes. Our job was to put the pieces in baskets, carry them to the attic, and stack them for the winter; it was a lot of work as well as hard. The house had five wood stoves: they had several purposes, they produced heat during the cold season, one in our kitchen to cook with a container for hot water on the side which was also used for our bath in a big tin bucket, had also an incorporated oven; the same one was in the grandparents kitchen, then we had three ceramic ones built in three bedrooms, they were wood stoves, tall, handsome with a door on the bottom to feed the stove with wood pieces, another door above to keep our copper water bottle warm to put in our bed to make it cozy. The builder of the wood stoves was the German friend who helped father during the time he was in forced labor, then emigrated to Alsace, settled near our home, they had a very strong relationship; I learned later; he kept father's earned money from his work, safely, when father would come home and go through the customs they would take it from him, so he told his German friend about it, the solution was to keep it in Germany until the liberation. That was the deal, it was good, father needing it, coming home to a wife and two children; so they were friends all their life; that day our task was to help, to contribute, we, the children, were happy to stack the wood, it was something new.

Father was very popular and good looking, his green eyes sparkling with life. He was always positive, joking, and on the go. He was a musician playing for the city, a marching band, and a festival two weekends in July (tangos, marches, waltzes). He became president of the soccer team, played billiards, bet on horses, was involved in politics, and generally full of life. He walked or biked everywhere, went to the butcher to choose his cuts of meat, and on Sunday as a treat he would take us to the patisserie in town where we could get a scoop of any flavored ice cream we wanted. We were happy. It was special going with Father, walking the four of us. I was very proud to be his daughter. I have memories to last a lifetime. My father became my idol. When I was seven I compared him to other parents. I thought mine looked like a movie star. I respected him. He was very strict with us. With me being the eldest, I had to perform in sports. Whatever I was involved in, I had to be number one. My brother was his favorite. He was the continuation of the last name, but I was his pride. His eye contact, smiles, and nodding (just for me) encouraged me in what I was doing. My parents were not affectionate. They didn't kiss us, tuck us in bed, or any of that wonderful love, warmth, security, togetherness, being-here-for-you stuff. It was survival. My siblings had it easier. My parents had plenty to deal with regarding my combative nature.

We had a pretty good routine. Every Saturday, Mother would put a big tin bucket on a bench in the kitchen, fill it with some boiling water from the wood stove, and mix it with cold water until it reached the right temperature. I had the privilege to go first, then my sister, Annick. My brother, Francis, was washed in the sink. When we were finished, Father helped Mother carry the bucket outside to dump the water in the canal.

In the spring, Father brought us kids — even my baby brother — to his friend, a shoemaker, to make us sandals. He measured our feet, and we chose the style. The color was brown, period. In the fall, we made another trip to get some shoes for the winter, they added a booty if we had snow, a shoe above our ankles with laces, I hated them, it was a lot of work to take them off, or to put them on. We were excited to have new shoes. We jumped up and down and pirouetted.

He also bought us slippers to switch to, and we lined our shoes neatly at the entrance. We were happy.

The teachers at my elementary school were Catholic nuns — sisters. Every day from 8:00 a.m. to 9:00 a.m. we had religion, which I skipped. Then we had the regular courses: French, history, geography, math, civics, music, and gymnastics. When we were outstanding, as a reward, we got a golden medal pin on our shirt for a week. When I got it I was proud, and my father even more. People would acknowledge it, since everybody knew us. It was a big deal.

I loved the holidays! Christmas was my favorite. There was something special in the air. People had smiles, everybody was in a festive mood, and the stores were very busy selling goods just for the season. They decorated with branches of holly and evergreens, leaving an everlasting smell. It was cold outside, the days were shorter, and all the houses had lights on. I loved it! A shiver of joy would go through my body. We often had a light supper, usually a soup with a buttered piece of bread, and zoomed to bed. With my mouchi under my chin, I quickly fell asleep. Meanwhile, my parents and grandparents brought in a big evergreen tree, put it in the dining room on the second floor, and dressed it with ornaments of that era, mostly handmade. The lights were small white candles in their holders, put on very carefully to avoid a fire. The room was rearranged, and when they were done, Mother woke us up. Half asleep, in our pyjamas, forgetting it was Christmas Eve, we went downstairs to the dining room. The scene was unreal. A tree in all its beauty with small packages, many of them, lying around it. The lights in the room were off, making it even more magical. I was stunned and tried to take in as much as I could. It was so beautiful. I rushed to inspect the ornaments, discovering them, amazed at how delicate, precious, and colorful they were. Then after we performed — reciting a poem, telling a story — Grandfather gave out one gift at a time, prolonging the pleasure of receiving. Our parents had a glass of glögg, a drink made especially for the Christmas holidays, and then we went back to bed.

The next day we would go back to our presents and play. Mother, preparing our fancy Christmas meal, watched us play, a serene look irradiating her face. She prepared an elaborated table setting with delicate china, crystal glasses, and silverware. Then she concentrated on the making of the meal: oysters; a pheasant, goose, or quails; mashed potatoes, snow peas, salad, cheese, and desert. She usually made a buche de Noel — a very rich pastry molded as a log, the elderly usually topped it with wine from Grandfather's vineyard. The feast was elaborate and special; it was a very happy time.

Another surprise! It was snowing! Little white flakes came from the sky in a whirlwind of tiny cotton balls that melted in our hands. Everything looked immaculate, untouched, a still picture. The culmination of Christmas was unreal. Grandfather had a sled stored in the attic, which he quickly retrieved, put us on it, and then pushed it down the hilly road in front of the house. We engaged in a snowball fight, our red faces smiling. When we got tired we went in, leaving our wet boots outside under the stoop and shaking our snowy clothes. We ran to the wood stove, finding the best spot, and enjoyed the warmth going up our spines.

One Christmas my sister and I got roller skates; what a wonderful way to travel! I went everywhere I could roll, finding out very fast that dirt roads were a no no.

The days went by, our parents took care of their schedules, and we went to school. I would get up early, study, and do my homework. My mind still fresh from my reading, ready for a dissertation, for an exchange of ideas. I was very aggressive and knew what I was taking about.

The days became a longer and warmer, and rain damped our earth, a musty smell rising and awakening nature. Birds flying, singing, building their nests, the sky brighter. Plants and trees budding, reborn. I was ready to venture on a new horizon, challenging whatever came my way.

As I grew older I had two good friends. After school we'd have a snack, do homework, have free time, and be back home by 5:30 p.m. at our places at the dinner table. Father was at the head, I was on his right, my sister next, on the left was my brother and then mother. The stove behind her keeping the food warm. Father was always served first. We couldn't leave our seats until we finished our plates, or asked for second servings, to be excused. I disliked spinach very much, and left it on my plate. Mother served me the same spinach on the same plate for a week. By that time it was black and dry. Finally I gave up, knowing I had no alternative, so I ate it. After that experience, I looked forward to tasting the green vegetable.

On Sunday my sister and I had to set the dining room table with a starched, white, cotton tablecloth and napkins. We'd use the formal china, which had Alsacien scenes on it. It was very colorful, interesting, and historic. The fluted crystal glasses were so fine and delicate, and Mother had bought the flatware in Paris. The whole ensemble was a delight to the eyes. We were ready for Easter.

The sun was bright, everything was green, and flowers were everywhere. Refreshing. Nature was reborn and I loved it, inhaling deeply and exhaling joyfully. We had new clothes, new shoes, and our hair combed — my curls were shoulder length and shiny. On Good Friday we went to church. This was the only time of the year we got communion — one piece of brioche and a drop of red wine to represent the body of Christ. For Protestants in Europe this was the most important day of the year. We prayed and reflected on our year — the good and the bad. Most businesses were closed until Monday.

The next day, Saturday, we colored the hard-boiled eggs Mother had cooked in the morning. We had little cups of different colors, paint brushes, and water, sitting around the kitchen table trying our artistry. It was fun, laughing at each other, my brother disturbing the process. After all the eggs were done, we went outside and played hopscotch.

Sunday was Easter, and festivity was in the air; life was good. We went to Sunday school. We walked to the Lutheran Church located on the other side of town and learned about the Ten Commandments. I often had arguments with my pastor, asking questions he couldn't answer. Religion often puzzled me. It was not like history, physics, algebra, or geometry where we had facts, theorems.

On our way home, we stopped at the corner of the Main Street waiting for the religious Catholic procession to come by. It was very colorful and dramatic — a man carrying a cross, a crown made out of twigs with thorns adoring his head. It ended with the city marching band in navy blue uniforms, sounds blasting from their instruments, playing a religious theme. My father played a sterling silver baryton, I was impatient trying to get a glimpse of him. Then we went home knowing we were going to look for a basket or a nest with eggs and goodies. It was always outside along

the canal and the house. We had a small garden with two
fruit trees, vegetables, herbs, and a row of roses — Father's
babies. Since we had just come out of winter, the vegetation
was small, easy to detect a nest or a basket. They were all the
same: candies shaped as eggs, chocolate roosters, and a lamb
in a fluffy cake. Our parents and grandparents watched us,
guiding us by saying, "hot" or "cold." They helped my little
brother a bit more. The smells coming from the kitchen
made us hungry. It was a feast for a prince: a leg of lamb
with flageolais (a white bean) flavored with garlic and herbs;
Father's mash with a rich, tasty sauce; salad; and desert,
a chocolate soufflé. We were thrilled, all together happy,
enjoying a beautiful table, a fantastic meal, and great wine
from the vineyard (for the adults).

We all had an agenda. While we were in school on
Monday's, it was laundry day for Mother. Across the bridge
opposite the canal the hospital added a covered space
with a basin and running water. It was a public place for
washing, so Mother used to bring a wooden board, a big
piece of brown soap (savon de Marseille), and the laundry
in a basket. She washed the clothes on her knees, using the
board, brushing the dirt with a rough brush, rinsing it in
the running water, and bringing the wet laundry home to
spread on a rope outside. A light wind and the sun would
dry them. Afterward the clothes smelled so delicious. In the
winter the laundry was cold and stiff. Between this place and
the house for the elderly there was a long, low building called
public baths (there were no houses that had bathtubs or
showers at that time). There were ten private rooms with one
or two bathtubs in it. A nurse dressed in white collected the
money and gave us a number. My sister, Annick, and I used
one room with two tubs. After sanitizing the tubs, the lady

started the water, adding some pine oil for an extra fee. We enjoyed it very much. Such a treat to have clean clothes on our backs, smelling good.

Cernay expanded and businesses were popping. People had jobs; everybody was eager to work. Down the street a Laundromat opened, so Mother went there. Father's business grew too. He was so busy he was named the best around town for his talent, quickness, joviality, and kindness, always there to help. He became very popular; it reflected on our lives.

Coming home from school I discovered a refrigerator, under the counter, 4 feet tall, the only one very happy was my mother; she was in heaven. The next wonder was a washer and a press — two rollers gliding over the sheets. All these appliances were rare in most of the household, so we were very surprised and curious. One day a week Blanche came to clean and iron a mountain of laundry. I loved to sit across from her, watch, and inhale the smell of a fresh, clean laundry.

Then an amazing black box, called the telephone, arrived. The ringer scared me. It was like Father was talking to a machine, putting his finger in one of the spaces, turning it until it stopped, letting go, and starting again with another number. Father was the only one using it. The calls were rare, only for business or communicating with Mittelwhir.

Father, at the height of his career, was in demand everywhere. We saw him less and less, usually only during our meals, some evenings, and of course mornings. Sunday was family time, from lunch on. He started an opera membership for Mother and me. He knew it was very special; after all, she had no fun time. Once a week, she had the radio on listening to classical music and opera. The city leased a bus on the marketplace to bring us to the large city of Mulhouse, where the opera house was located. It was a big event. We got dressed up. I was in heaven! I saw and heard the world's most famous singers: Maria Callas, Renata Tebaldi, Mario Lanza, Enrico Caruso. Powerful voices resounded through this beautiful theater. How humbling it was to listen, to be part of it, to enjoy it, the drama, the tragic endings, the sorrow. I was always torn by the beauty and the cruel endings, so dramatic. My wheels spun between love and hate. The music was also so deep, possessive. The stages were always very elaborate, breathtaking. I was in another world. This was the type of evening I truly enjoyed. Father gave me the moon. My thoughts often went to the drama of relationships, love, hate, and murder. I started to know the classical melodies and would sing them. It made Father very happy; classical music was his thing. Sometimes Mother would take me to a ballet, instead of an opera. I was fascinated by the scenery, the agility, the weightlessness, and the prowess of these dancers. How graceful, lovely to watch. At night I would dream about *Swan Lake, Sleeping Beauty, Nutcracker*, and *Gisele*. I would dance, swirl, jump, become one of them. From then on I wanted to be a ballet dancer. All this became part of the mold that shaped me, as well as classical music. It will always be a part of me.

Father smoked like a chimney. One day he decided to stop cold turkey. We didn't think too much about it. One Monday he called us outside and introduced us to a brand-new black car, a Peugeot 202. I couldn't believe my eyes. A car! My grandparents were uncertain about it. They wondered, *Why this big machine!* They figured we didn't need it. We were the third family in town to own one. We hopped in it, feeling and smelling the untouched cream-colored leather. It was a treat to sit in it. Father took us for a ride, spinning around the corner. It was a surprise, even Mother didn't know. Father used the car to go to Mittelwhir to Grandmama's house or to go to his meetings or practices out of town. His car was his baby, his most cherished acquisition, and he pampered it. Pierrot, one of his best friends, was a mechanic managing the top garage in town, so everything was under control. He knew people everywhere: different class levels, politicians, clergy, people in finance.

The country was coming back to life with its political machine. Businesses took off, and people made money and improved their lives. Early in 1952, going to school at my regular time (nine o'clock), I noticed a hostile atmosphere. My classmates looked at me strangely, differently. At ten o'clock we had a break. We gathered in the court and played, when suddenly a student threw stones at me and called me a heretic. I tried to avoid the hits, not knowing what was happening, not understanding the situation, or what to do about it. When I got hit on my nose, I bled profusely. It scared me so I ran home, putting my hand over my face in pain. Father took one look at me, then his watch to see if he had time to go to the other school and knew what and why this happened. The nuns had brained washed the kids. After my bleeding was under control, Father brought me to Cours Complementaire — a co-ed public school that was part college level. The president of the school listened to my father. If I passed the test, I was more than welcome to attend. There was a lot of pressure on me. My father's pride was at stake. I passed the test with flying colors and became the youngest student. There were only five in my class (most parents sent their children to work at the factories to bring money home).

I was ready for the new school year. I got a briefcase (it was a statement), new books, a fountain pen, and lots of notepads with specific subjects written on each cover. It was exciting! Our program included arithmetic, algebra, geometry, literature, theology, chemistry, physics, music, gymnastic, art, and German as a second language. I embraced most of them. I had to get used to cohabitating with boys. I had a brother with whom I had no affinity. He was there as part of the family, but we had such a different life with five years apart during our adolescence. Boys to me were scary, different, an unknown field I never thought of it. During my time with the nuns at elementary school there were never talks of gender, how we were different. I had no clue. Day by day I got more acquainted with my classes, stayed away from playing, and studied very hard to be among the top. One of my favorite times at school was in gymnastics. My professor would throw me in the air and make me perform flips and other gymnastic moves. Some students had a hard time with it. I had the highest scores in class. But one time during a regional contest, at the end of my run across the track I collapsed. Our family doctor detected a heart murmur, so there was no more gymnastics for me. I was very disappointed.

I had a bike and I had one friend down the street. I talked to him occasionally when we ran into each other. My father was against our friendship. Gabriel was my buddy. He had long, loose, black curly hair that framed an amazing face, two black-as-coal eyes, full lips, white sparkling teeth, and tanned skin. With his Italian heritage, he came from a family with many siblings. I was very particular about looks; I liked only beautiful people and nice surroundings. When it came to food, I smelled everything. If I didn't like it, I wouldn't try it nor taste it.

Sunday, we packed the car early in the morning, skipping Sunday school, and headed for Mittelwhir to visit Mother's family. We watched the scenery, since there were few cars on the road. The mountains were far away, their uneven summit meeting the sky with arrogance, overlooking the valley. There was a castle here and there. I was always amazed by the history of these impressive fortresses. Then we went by hills of vineyards, and we knew then we were getting close. It was very picturesque, colorful, giving you a feeling of richness. As we entered the village, there were high brick walls built along the main road, and behind them a big main house that had a huge cellar with stacks of labeled bottles of wine harvested from their estate. Plus they had different buildings — not destroyed by war — used for business. The Germans loved French wines: white, red, rose, champagne. We left the main road to drive on dirt roads. We discovered a different scene. The government, after the Liberation, gave each family one barrack on their lot. They were wooden rectangular boxes with few windows (one level) with an outhouse. The Germans had raided the entire village, burning everything standing, even the church where people took refuge. There were no identification papers left, no pictures, no memories, nothing. On the lower part of the town there were remains, what were at one time homes.

We arrived to at Grandmama's house. The family hugged each other; it was happy time. Everybody had survived the war except one, Emile. We never knew what, when, or where he lost his life. They had a big garden, a chicken coop, and the vineyards with some fruit trees. Grandmama received us as well as Amelie, Mother's youngest sister. There was also one brother, Andre, who had settled in a barrack down the road. The rest of the family was scattered, wherever they had found work. We always had great meals, harvested from their land; it was fresh, organic. We helped to get water down the dirt road, pumping the spigot, filling the tin buckets, and carrying them up to the barracks, which became their home for many years. There was no electricity; instead, kerosene lamps and wooden stoves were used during the cold months. They were also used for cooking. A butane bottle was used for heating some meals in the summer. We were happy! No rules, playing outside, the place was all ours, everything easy. It was called relaxed time. Summer was here, with it outings. One Sunday, a gathering of people from the Music Band leased a bus and a driver, and we went to the mountains, the Vosges, to spend the day outside playing games, having meals at a restaurant outside under huge umbrellas, and listening to music blasting. Father took my hand, swept me to the dance floor, and taught me how to follow the beat, the sound. I learned something new, a lot of fun, freedom of movement. I was in a different world. Now I understood Father's love for music; it was his escape from everyday life. Also, he was an unbelievably outstanding dancer! From then on, whenever I had the opportunity to dance, I took it.

Fall started, which meant the harvesting of grapes. A group of Father's friends came to help. They climbed the steep hills of the vineyard with baskets on their backs and a shear in one hand. The grapes were collected in a barrel, then put into a press. A clear liquid went into a clean bottle where it was corked and labeled. The reward was to gather around a huge table, drinking the wine from last year, enjoying Mother's potato salad with sausages, having animated conversation, laughing loudly, and singing old songs resounding from the walls to ceiling! A few weeks later, some of the group met again to make snaps, a clear alcohol made from fruits, two types, mirabelle and quesch (a small plum) it was very strong but tasty, fruity with a distinctive aroma.

I rode my bike, zooming around the corner, the wind caressing my face, my nose up smelling the roses, my hair flying. It felt so good. I was on my way to get Father, reminding him it was time for dinner. As I approached the building on the outskirts of town, I could smell a strong odor; he was processing the fruits to make alcohol. As I entered, there were huge, shiny copper containers with piping everywhere, very impressive, overwhelming. An intense fire fueled the process. I was very interested in learning how the fruit went through the alembics to become a crystal clear liquid. A tasty, digestive and after-dinner delight. Grandfather and Father were the makers of this elixir. It was consumed with respect, slowly, enjoying the flavor and taste, relishing the fruits of their labor. They stored it on shelves in the cellar; the bottles were labeled and dated. It was tasted only on special occasion. The tradition stopped after Father's death; the grandfather clause had ended.

I was about twelve, and one day Father called the three of us and asked us which one took 5.00 Franc. equivalent to 5.00 $. He always had a lot of change in his pockets. We looked at each other and nobody came forward. The weeks went by. In a few days we would celebrate Christmas. As was the custom, we went to bed around eight o'clock. In the morning, Mother woke us up. We jumped out of bed, went down the staircase two steps at a time, and arrived at the dining room. We discovered a pyramid of citrus covering the entire table. Where was the tree? The presents? Father greeted us with these words: "Who took my 5.00 Franc?" We looked at each other. Silence! He said, "Therefore somebody is lying. This is your Christmas, and you being the oldest, it was probably you. You are going to write 500 times: I don't lie, before the end of the week." I couldn't believe what I was hearing! A punishment for something I didn't do! I knew I had no way out. I couldn't confront my Father without proof. I still had no clue who it was! I didn't mind being punished for something I did, but this was too much. A shimmering anger took place within me; I was fuming. I wrote many times: I don't lie. When I presented the paper to my father, who counted each line, I was short of five. He told me to write 500 times: I don't cheat. Now I looked very guilty. Time went by, and I had forgotten about the incident, when my sister said, "With the 5.00 Franc I got this." (I forgot what it was.) I never forgave her for not coming forward, after this incident my relationship with her was distant and the one with my father was a little different.

The school year came to a close, and my parents decided to send me to a summer camp. It would be a good experience for me to be in a different environment; it would broaden my horizon. So they enrolled me in a camp south of France. I went with my mouchi, my friend. I knew few children. I never was away from my family; it was very scary to me. The complex was not far from the beach, on the Mediterranean Sea. The camp had simple buildings, and there were forty of us with few adults. The days were filled with games, plays, music, theater, learning to swim, and building sand castles. I was very shy, watching, listening, aloof. For some reason, the supervisor liked me, protected me, looked after me. We developed a friendly relationship, and we had deep talks about life. She understood my fears, my loneliness, and lack of love at home. So one day, while playing on the beach — going into the cold water, jumping against the waves — three girls came up on me, put my head under the water, and held it. Finally, my supervisor saw the commotion and came to my rescue, but they had to perform CPR. It was not my time, yet it added another fear in my life. Now I was claustrophobic and had a water phobia.

Back home, I never mentioned anything, but it was the last time I went to camp. Every year on the last weekend in June, and first in July, we had a festival. Trailers came and drifters settled on the ground of the Grun (the park) and set up their stands. The city built a big dance floor with an elevated, covered stage for the band. The city promoted this type of entertainment to generate funds, business, and to bring people together, young and old. We all looked for those happy times. The music blasted from the stands after 7:00 p.m., bringing smiles to many faces on the dance floor. Father was part of the four people playing music, entertaining the dancers. For little money, you could buy a shot toward a target, get a stuffed animal, see a fortune teller, the magician, the rides, and the bumping cars (auto box as we called them). My parents gave my sister and me some money, not a lot, but we were pleased to get something and enjoy the afternoon. My duty as the eldest was to look after my siblings no matter our disagreements, we made sure we stayed together; I never trusted the crowd. Though one time, my sister went for a ride, I waited, and when she passed in front of me a young man was with her in the car. Being surrounded by strangers, we looked after each other (our instinct).

I spent most of July in Mittelwhir at my grandmother's place. My two cousins were also there: Jacqueline, four years my elder; Georgette, two years my elder. For many years we were together on vacation. We got along and had fun. One room at the back of the barrack had a window looking out onto the garden. The room had three twin beds and a nightstand. Grandmama had the room next to the front door, which led to a room with a sink, a wood stove with two burners over a butane bottle, a big wooden table with two long benches, a wall stand holding metal plates and cups, and two drawers for flatware. It was very rustic, simple. We were happy to get water, to stack wood under a protected space from the rain, pick vegetables in the garden for the meals, and check the chicken coop for eggs.

Uncle Andre had a barrack down the road on a very small lot. He was the warden checking all the hills around us for trespassing, hunting, or stealing; it was a huge responsibility. He'd be on foot all day long, carrying a shot gun, checking the land with his binoculars. He married an Italian, Aunt Denise. She was very pretty with long, black, loose curls; big black eyes; and a beautiful smile. She was very shy, outnumbered by her sisters-in-law who didn't care for her. She had good taste, elegant, and made anything look great out of nothing. A very good cook. She knew how to entertain, and my uncle adored her; we liked each other very much. I visited her every day during my stay. Grandmama took care of the barrack, made our beds, our meals, and Aunt Amelie helped her. In the mornings the rooster woke us up. A little later a big man with a red face and a bullhorn informed us of the local news, important things regarding our nation; there was no radio. I thought this was exciting. I used to stand outside and listen to him. Then we'd go to the vineyard and pick fruit and climb trees. Everything was fun; we all loved it. We also helped pick some vegetables to store for the winter; nothing was wasted.

Down the road a very good-looking young man lived with his parents, across from Uncle Andre. Many girls went after him; He was a good catch. He noticed Aunt Amelie, who was demure, aloof, and hardworking. He asked her out, and after a short courtship he asked her if she would marry him. She said yes. We were all happy! So then Uncle Eric came into the family, he became a beloved uncle. Three weeks goes by fast when you are having fun. Soon it was time to get ready for school.

Before Tonton, Tata, my father's brother and my mother's sister and their two children Jacqueline, Roger headed back to Paris, they would give us beautiful clothes — to me from Jacqueline, and to Francis from Roger. The dresses were well made, very stylish, outstanding. We loved it because they came from Paris! They also had a good time, away from the hustle and bustle of Paris routine, away from a structured life to freedom, playing outside every day. When the sun went down we would take walks around town, learning about the constellations. I was fascinated by Tonton; he knew about a lot of things. On Sunday, we would go to the mountains, the Vosges. It was beautiful up there. The valley looked like it had small villages, houses gathering like a fist, adding bright colors, the castles hanging on their cliffs, the forests, and of course the fresh air. Breathtaking. They would find a spot to park the two cars — the Peugeot and the Panhard — get the blankets and picnic baskets out, and we would climb a little hill until we found the right view, the best setting. Our grandparents were always included; they enjoyed their sons and family. We played petanque and volleyball. The fresh air and plenty of exercise rejuvenated the elderly, and we burned our lasting energy.

The country was coming back to life, and with it the political machine. Businesses took off, people made money and improved their lives. One evening, we were in bed when we heard a huge commotion downstairs. My sister and I shared the same room on the third floor. We crawled out of bed, and slowly and silently went down one floor. We stuck our heads between the handrail bars and saw Father going into the kitchen with a bloody face, limping. We wondered what happened. My sister was too young and had no clue. I learned that Father was campaigning for the socialist party and got hit. That was the end of his political aspiration, with our blessings. Grandfather was the only one discontent and upset; his fanatical beliefs started to crumble. We never liked each other anyway. The elders were just thinking about how to shape the world, we, bringing us under their political wing, promising equality, a better life; grandfather belong to a group recruiting people to the Soviets. After World War II communism was the solution; the German's rules still to this day are in effect, voting, banking, taxes, laws in general. When Father had meetings in the house — in the evenings when we were supposed to be a sleep — my mind was always working, hearing unusual noises. I was curious and wanted to know! Little by little I developed my own opinion. I was not so sure about Father's philosophy to be equal, everybody having the same thing. So one day I encountered him and asked, "Why do we have a car? You should share." He answered, "I worked for it." It didn't satisfy me.

The school year started. The Parisians went back to the big city, and we returned to our normal routine. Mother knew how to sew, knit, crochet; it was a very important part of our grooming. We had to be self-sufficient. So at school we had a project each week, which took care of some of our free time. I crocheted my own coat, knitted multiple sweaters, tops, and stitched needlepoint on many tablecloths. I still have some.

One summer my parents sent me to Aunt Fanny (number four of Mother's siblings) for two weeks. Their children were around my age: Albert, Georgette, and Suzanne, the eldest. They lived in Mundolsheim, near Stasbourg. It was a bigger city than Cernay, a region where they made a famous beer. They had a big house on a busy street with a lot of movement. We also were busy. It was the season for picking the hops from the field, separating the flowers from the stems, selecting them, and putting them in different baskets. We would earn twenty-five cents per basket. At the end of the stay, I brought home 5 Franc or 5 $ to add to my bank. I had the opportunity to go to a brewery and watch them make beer. It was cool.

One day my father decided to cut my hair. It was short and I hated it. I felt naked. I felt like I lost my identity, a part of my soul, like Samson. My power, my looks, my life became more and more difficult at home. I was a teenager now, tall, thin, looking differently. Father became very possessive, taking my space away, my freedom. My Father's friends were watching me, checking me out. It upset me because I didn't do anything wrong. I had no boyfriend, I was not hanging around, I always was an outsider, and I became very irritable, arguing a lot. On Sunday afternoon, with Father's approval, we could see a movie in the only theater in town. We could sit anywhere, so my sister and I usually went to the balcony, sometimes Gabriel snuck and sat next to me. One time he took my hand, and shivers went down my spine. For the first time somebody, a male, showed me affection. I was thrilled! I didn't think too much about it because I was busy with school. He wrote me poems; I was very touched.

I was fifteen, finishing my last year of school and biking on my free time. Life was good. That year, during the annual fair, I met a young man who was seventeen. I thought he was so handsome, much taller than me, green eyes, a lot of straight black hair, great smile, and very pleasant. There were many stands, offering anything out of your norm, just for fun and the unexpected. He started to question me about games, shooting stand where he got me a bear. We spent time going to places. Suddenly, he put his hands in my hair, pulled me toward him, and our eyes locked. He hugged me, grazed my lips with his, and it startled me. I ran home and washed my mouth. I kept it secret. I was changed, something unknown had happened to me, and it bothered me. I couldn't talk to anyone about it; my father would kill me. The difference between Gabriel whom I liked very much and Bruno whom I was attracted to made me insecure. He lived in the next town, biking up and down the hills to try to see me. We never just ran into each other. My life was taking a different path.

32

I ended my last year of school, passing my final test, and getting my diploma. The Brevet. The president of the school had an interview with my father about my future, suggesting I would be a terrific architect. After reviewing my last year of school, my designs were all over the classroom. My father became numb. All he could see was his brother's experience, the hardship it caused the family during and after the war. Meanwhile, my father was exchanging ideas about my future with his brother. His reasoning, there is always work for a hairstylist during war time or peace. He decided how I should go to the best cosmetology school in Paris for two years, graduate, and come back home. His goal was to open a chain of hair salons, train the personnel, and oversee the operation. He never mentioned to me his dream. He got in touch with the school, enrolled me, and paid the tuition, which was very high, equal to any private institution. One evening my father told me about his plans; Mother sat next to him. I listened. I liked the idea of living in Paris; it suited me very well. I didn't object. They saw that I was content, so the deal was made. A few days later I packed a small suitcase, including my beloved mouchi, and hopped in the car next to Jacqueline. When we arrived in Paris, I was in awe. It was so beautiful, driving close to the monuments, the buildings, the parks, the trees, the traffic, so many cars, so many pedestrians, so much life, vibrant, everything new to discover. I was very excited and knew I was on my way to a new chapter in my life.

Life was animated on 16 Rue Levis, the address of my uncle and aunt, tonton and tata, it's famous and very well known for its open market. Twice a week merchants put their stands up and sold their goods. By 1:00 PM the street was clear, leaving no trace of early business. The building, where my family lived, had a big, wooden double door, a dark hall, and a concierge watching, checking who came and went. A staircase winding up to the tenth floor. There were two doors; the one on the left was ours. As we entered a small apartment greeted us. There was a small kitchen on the left, a short hall giving way to a dining room with a sofa, one bedroom with a bathroom, shower, bidet, and at the end of the hall a toilet. Everything was harmonious, serene, family-like, well decorated, and practical. Tonton would come home for lunch. Tata straightened the apartment, did the laundry, ironing, went to the market, and cooked. Jacqueline, Roger went to their schools, I went to the cosmetology school. I took the metro, had to change stations, and walk to the school, I had to learn to get my pass, be careful not to talk to strangers, be aware of my surroundings, and keep my money safe from the pickpockets.

I had many classes. Every Monday we had to go to a museum to study everything about an era, including their hairdos, and write a report. From Tuesday to Friday we had classes, practice, and discussions. On Thursday we had math, business, accounting, interacting with people, diplomacy, and a foreign language. It was a very busy, interesting, and challenging schedule. On Saturday we were assigned to work in a hair studio, watch, help, and write a memo about our experience. So I had the opportunity to visit and participate in the top shops. I became very involved, putting my mind and soul into it. I learned fast, and more than requested. My new world became very important. I could show my artistry, improve looks, and make things beautiful. I had good knowledge of hair-coloring chemistry, the effects of minerals in the body and on the hair, and interacting with people from different backgrounds. This yielded conversations about art, fashion, books, news, knowing were to fit, politeness, and humility.

We had practice a few days a week. People would come and wait to be selected as a model. I would get the same person each time. She had a nice head of hair and charming personality. We paid them per session, and my model was patient, encouraging me when I was frustrated. We were a good pair. She was my mother's age, I respected and liked her. These ladies had financial hard times, some were homeless, they looked for any opportunity to make little money, to feel good and to cover their humble expenses. At the cosmetology school I made two friends, Jean and Jacques B. Very different. Jean was shy, low key, gentle, smiling, always helping. Jacques was flamboyant, burly, forceful, black hair and eyes, and roaring; you couldn't miss him. I liked his frankness and boldness. We worked side by side, exchanged ideas and projects, and interacted with each other. Going home from school, taking the metro during rush hour, we were all squeezed, trying to stay stable as the train stopped and started, trying to be safe when wandering hands tried to touch us. I was always happy to get to my uncle's house. Around the table our discussions were always very interesting. Jacqueline studied biology, and Roger studied engineering, specializing in nuclear. Tonton was an architect, I was in cosmetology, and everything revolved around Tata who was our stable rock. She coordinated our schedules and made everything easy. It was a different life, all new tasks; I grew up quite fast.

On Sundays, all together enjoying our weekend morning, we'd walk to the Lutheran Church. Then we had lunch after we dressed the table — steaks and french fries were usually on the menu, everybody's favorite. Then we'd go to a park or to the country to play games (horseshoe, volleyball, whatever) to breathe in the fresh air and have some exercise. Afterward we'd head home tired and happy.

The quarters were tight. We were growing up, becoming adults, each one reaching their goal. We needed more space. Later on, my uncle found a room to rent on the eleventh floor, not far from the staircase. That level was to lodge maids, often students, and there was one only bathroom — shower, sink, toilet — in the hall to share. My small room had a big window. We put in a single bed, which I transformed into a couch, a small table with a lamp, a hanging folding storage, and a white rug. I was happy. I decorated my room with posters and curtains for privacy. I had my shower, my meals — breakfast and dinner — and socializing downstairs. Tonton had a lot of wisdom and serenity; it warmed my heart. Finally I felt at home. I embraced it fully.

We had wonderful teachers who won national prizes, contests, or were retired and went into teaching. We were in good hands. They even looked after us since we were so young. I wanted to be named Nicky to commemorate my new life; I had turned a page. I was on a tight budget but would bring a baguette, some ham, and gruyere to share. Sometimes I would have lunch with Jean and Jacques in a small bistro to celebrate something. They were my best friends, and I could trust them. Sometimes I was their model when we were short. I learned from them, and they learned from me.

Paris became my beloved city. I was very familiar with the metro. I became observant, vigilant, not so friendly on the street, and I rarely took a cab. I walked a lot trying to save money for purchases. I made it with what I had and was happy.

By my second year of school I was still loving it. I became the top student, and life at Tonton's was rewarding, I had a warm home and became very close to my family. I was very, very happy, and life was fantastic. I also noticed men would look at me. What else could I ask for? On holidays, Christmas and Easter, I would take the regular train — and eight-hour ride — to get to my parents' house. Father would be at the train station in Mulhouse waiting for me with a big smile on his face, his arms open. Then we had to drive another twenty-five minutes. Mother would greet me in front of the house, so happy to see me. They found I had changed, matured. I was outspoken, didn't wait anymore to be asked to speak and little by little shedding the layers of my childhood. I was never close to my parents, so they were even more surprised to discover their child, who they never knew. I had become estranged from my sister and brother. The combination of country and city living broadened my knowledge, my cleverness. I isolated myself, became more aloof, independent, living in my own bubble where I was comfortable and secure. My books were my universe. I was happy to be home, to be with my siblings trying to connect. My brother, older now, admired me. I was his big sister. He looked up to me, and I became his idol. My sister and I never were on the same page. She wanted to topple me, with no luck, either academically or physically; there was always rivalry. Mother protected her all the time; she was her security. My sister was the cry baby. Now that I was living in Paris the gap widened. Being in the hair business you deal with fashion, you conduct yourself differently, and you dress better even with less money. Wherever I went I stood out, people treated me with respect, and my sister started to resent me. I didn't pay too much attention to it. I just accepted things as they were. I didn't have time to look into it since I was there for a short visit.

I wanted to go to Mittelwhir to see Grandmama and Aunt Amelie; they represented my fun time, vacation, very few rules, sooo sooo nice. There the family always compared me to Aunt Mariette, number nine of the siblings. We had similar hair (blondish reddish color), loose curls, nice body, good posture, style, and smarts. She was working for a psychologist at that time. They said we were wild horses, independent, unorthodox. Time spent at home was nice; after all, it was my family, but I couldn't wait to go back to my tiny room and Tonton's family.

Before long, Father and Mother brought me back to the train station in Mulhouse. I kissed and hugged them, hopped on the train, and put my window down to say good-bye one more time. As the train gained more speed, they became smaller and smaller, disappearing from my eyesight. I arrived at Gare de l'Est in Paris, took the metro to Villiers, the station next to Rue Levis where Tonton lived. Everybody was happy to see me and asked me about my stay, gathering around the dining table with animated conversation and great food. I really felt at home and had a very good night in my little room alone, no noise, recollecting my visit with my parents.

On Sunday morning the three of us — Jacqueline, Roger, and I — went to the Lutheran Church. They had a special program recreating a theological event called Andromaque. The group decided I ought to play the heroine. I knew the story, having studied it at school. I was too shy to say anything so I complied. I was going to be buried alive behind cemented walls, dying little by little, which made me uncomfortable. I was claustrophobic, but I kept quiet, deciding to be strong and hide my fear.

At school I was very busy. One day Jean asked me if I wanted to go to a party. His neighbor and friend were having a gathering on Sunday, but I didn't know what he was taking about! I never knew what a party was, at home we didn't have teenagers get together, I was curious. He assured me we would have fun. After lunch at Tonton's, I snuck out of my room, took a cab to Av. General Tripier. The building was outstanding. It was on a corner, part of the Champ de Mars, on the foot of the Eiffel Tower. I entered the heavy iron gate and glass double doors. On the right was an elevator, which was also in glass framed by wrought iron. Instead I took the wide steps in marble, carpeted with a red rug. I rung the bell at the designated door and somebody opened it. I entered into a large hall opening to the gathering. I looked around, unfamiliar to a young crowd. Glasses were in hands, music blasting, laughing, talking. I was shy in this unknown situation. There were a lot of people. I looked around, and my eyes locked onto a pair of green eyes, a young man with beautiful straight black hair, a dazzling smile, inviting. He took my hand and introduced himself as Jacques. He asked my name. "Nicky," I said. He took me around, introducing me to his brothers and some guests. When I finally spotted Jean, I was relieved. I was overwhelmed by the number of young people who easily interacted with each other. Jacques didn't leave me. He served me a drink and asked me questions about my life. I saw some people kissing, touching each other, lying on the sofa, and I panicked! When Jacques went to get something, I took the opportunity to grab my bag, exit the door, and hail a cab. That night I had a lot to think about! Jacques's face never left my thoughts. Something happened within me. Seeing the kissing and touching was new to me. I never saw my parents in that way, and there was none of that in the movies I watched. My parents, or teachers (nuns) in school, never mentioned sex. I felt stupid, uneducated. Who could I consult? I brushed away all my doubts and went on to my daily routine.

In the week, Jacques came to pick me up. Jean probably gave him the information. I was happily surprised! Seeing him at the entrance, waiting for me, my heartbeat quickened and my legs shook. I was never so happy to see somebody. He took my hand firmly, like he had known me forever. I melted inside, but looked stoic. We rode the metro close to each other and our eyes locked. When we got to my station, we walked to 16 Rue de Levis, where we kissed. Our lips touched very slightly and then we departed. I was astounded! Something had happened within me. I had to compose myself in front of my family and just casually talk about my day. My soul, heart, and brain were getting more and more involved with Jacques. I never experienced such a strong feeling. It was like a hurricane, an earthquake, within me. I had never asked myself what the difference was between a man and a woman. I didn't know! The conversation never came up. I was a little confused and insecure about the subject. Sometimes I would go to Rue du Quatre Septembre where he worked for a company editing daily cartoons and drawing humorous caricatures. I was curious and wanted to know more; I was drawn toward the unknown. Between school and Jacques I felt I needed a phone, so I saved my train fares and walked. Finally, I bought a phone. It was much easier to communicate.

Jacqueline met a young man at church, and they fell in love. She was blonde with blueish-greenish eyes, tall, always smiling, serene, optimistic, and classy. She reminded me a lot of Ingrid Bergman. Her boyfriend, Roland, was an only child with a domineering mother. Jacqueline was a very beautiful bride. They settled in the south in a small town, and got involved in church and the community. They had four children.

At the end of my second year of school, Jacques came to pick me up. We were laughing and teasing each other. His beautiful smile and full lips made me want to have more. Before departing he told me of a party in his parents' apartment the coming Sunday. The gathering included some of his friends whom I had met briefly before. With the music blasting, Jacques took me to his bedroom that had a half-moon window from where I could see the Eiffel Tower. Our eyes locked and he touched my lips with his fingers, a serious look upon his face. He kissed me while walking me to his bed where we fell. My head and body exploded. I was in heaven, feeling his hands all over me. Shyly I responded. Our clothes quickly dropped onto the rug. My pink nipples were exposed, standing straight up, hard, begging for more. Suddenly, there was a slight pain between my legs. Jacques kept kissing me, smiling, and not a word was exchanged. We were in our world, happy. When we got up, I noticed a soiled sheet. I was surprised and concerned, but Jacques reassured me that Antoinette would take care of it. I didn't know what had happened. A few days later, while discussing an article in the paper, I learned about losing your virginity. I had lost mine. I loved Jacques. I was his and that's all that mattered. Now, I was truly hooked. I was infatuated and he was my universe!

We were teenagers, discovering, trying new horizons, being independent, doing, going wherever.

It was a different society then. Nobody spoke about work. Work was secondary; fun was primary. I had a goal. I was going to make it on my own, better than my father, and nothing was going to change my path. Jacques had a group of friends with the same background — parents never home, wealthy, housekeepers looking over the children. If they ever got in trouble, they were always bailed out. They had no chores, plenty of money, and everything was on hand and easy. Jacques gave me the privilege of getting a taste of skiing, going to the Alps for a weekend, sunning on the beach of Normandy, Deauville, where we also took part in horse races and, the most exciting event, driving a Formula One race car on the tracks. We went to many places in Jacque's Vespa — a small motorcycle. I was astonishing at how so many different challenges could bring me so much pleasure and happiness. I was walking on air!

Our clan consisted of Yves, Laurent and Rosine (they were a couple), Jean, Jacques, Christian, plus a few others. We were like a big family who looked after each other. If we stayed overnight somewhere, we would take a room in a hotel, put two double beds together, snuggle next to each other and sleep. There was lots of laughing and joking. We were always on the go, nonstop, fun and more fun. One Sunday we went to Yves' parents' apartment. There was a full-sized painting of his mother on the wall, and it was stunning; she was a beauty. Her ninth husband was a movie producer. Jacques asked me to cook a meal. I complied. There were plenty of canned goods and food. After opening some of the cans I asked where to dispose of them. He told me to just put it in the sink and push the button, which

I did. It grinded to a stop. I never dealt with a garbage disposal, but I knew something went wrong. Jacques told me to just let it go. I didn't like to leave destruction behind me, but there was nothing I could do, so I let it go.

Another time we went to the Vallee of Chevreuse, at Cernay — the same name of my parents' town — to visit Jacques' friends. He was a painter, and she was a socialite. It was a beautiful town. It was nice to get away from the city. The town was charming with narrow streets, very picturesque, country houses with a touch of class! I loved it; there was no ostentation. I felt at home. We had a great time! I noticed Jacques flirting with Annie, the hostess. It was the first time I noticed something like this. I kept very close to him that night. Jean Jacques became ill from drinking too much and threw up all evening. The next day we were back on the scooters via Paris. We were "The Group," meeting at the Cafe Gare Saint Lazare outside on the sidewalk, around a few tables we pushed side by side. We sat sipping our beverages, wondering what our next move or destination was going to be. A middle-aged man listening to us suggested Joinville-Le-Pont, so we went. We ended up in a small town with the river Marne running through with barges. It was charming. It was a favorite spot for painters and artists; Maurice Chevalier was a regular. There was a man who was always around us. He seemed syrupy and I had a strange feeling. At that time there were people preying on young, wealthy teenagers, enticing them into porno groups. We always stayed as a party, never split, and protected each other. We were so very young, under twenty, beautiful, naïve, optimistic, and felt invincible. "The Group" always had money, having wealthy parents.

When we went to the movies, we girls wanted to watch movies that were very romantic and sensitive. Some actors impressed me more than others. In the category of handsome: Jean Marais, Alain Delon, Louis Jourdan, Charleston Heston, and Gregory Peck. For performances: Anthony Quinn, Jean Louis Philippe, Jean Paul Belmondo, and Bourvil. For actresses: Sophia Loren, Michele Morgan, Grace Kelly, Ingrid Bergman, and many more. Sometimes we went to listen to singers, like Dario Moreno, Gilbert Becaud, Brassens, Aznavour (our favorite), and Harry Belafonte. We would sing their tunes a lot and dance to Ray Charles songs, as well as Sidney Bechet, The Platters, and listen to Mahalia Jackson.

We went dancing at Rue de la Huchette at Le Bidule. We were impressed by three singers: Edith Piaf, Louis Armstrong, and Jacques Brel. We were at l'Olympia, a theater near the Madeleine, the top for entertainment! We went to see Edith Piaf. It was packed. The lights went off and only the stage had dimed lights. Here came a very little lady wearing a little black dress. She took the microphone, opened her mouth, and an unbelievable sound erupted with high notes and low notes, sometimes so sad, nostalgic. It went through my body. I was under her spell; she was controlling my emotions. I felt joy as well as sorrow. The sounds rebounded from wall to wall; it was an unforgettable evening. We were reduced to nothing but empty souls. She took everything away from us, overpowering our feelings. It was a memorable evening.

Another singer who impressed me very much was Louis Armstrong. We were always curious about Americans. Most of them became famous in France, so with all the publicity around his show, we decided to see him at

Rue de la Huchette, at the 2 Magots, a famous spot for singers. It was a small room with a stage, long wooden tables, and benches, they served drinks. A few musicians played, starting the prelude, and then it got louder when Louis Armstrong entered the stage. He was humungous, powerful. He started with jokes and then began to sing. His big mouth opened, rocking us with these beautiful songs. I wanted to jump up next to him and be hugged, swayed away. I wanted to stay next to him; he made me feel good! The audience sang and enjoyed every minute. He was like a big bear, warm, comfortable, with a huge smile. It was heartwarming.

Then I saw Jacques Brel, amazing! He was a phenomenon with overwhelming energy coming out of his long and skinny body. The cry, the happiness, the loneliness went through me and I related to him. I felt like him, the energy, the very highs, and the very lows. He ripped me apart, left me with no feelings, no soul, empty.

One weekend Jacques, one of his friends, and I went on a trip to Switzerland to ski. It was fun being away from the city. The snow-covered mountain was so impressive, cool, immaculate, white, breathtaking. In the evening we ended up at a disco. Jacques danced, flirted, and charmed young dancers, while I sat with his friend, watching, my stomach cramping from jealousy. It looked like a scene from the movie *Les Liaisons Dangereuses*. Then I got up and went to our room. I didn't want to think about tomorrow, couldn't face it. The next day we departed for home, driving up and down the winding roads. Jacques decided to stop. He wanted to find out how many drivers would react, so he lay in the middle of the road, as if he were just in an accident. Cars came by but no one stopped. Everybody could see it was a setup, no accident, no trace of rocks falling. Finally he got up, vexed, and went back to the car via Paris.

I knew my side of the family wouldn't, couldn't comprehend their type of living. The only recreation Tonton and others had was going outside of Paris or to a park to get a taste of fresh air, family time. My father was involved with soccer, billiards, music, and sometimes going to Mittelwhir to socialize with the family. A different life in different places. I never heard Jacques talk about his parents. I learned later his father was a builder (airports, sky resorts, buildings) and had something to do with banking. His mother was a champion in bridge and had played with Omar Sharif, a frequent partner. She won several tournaments. His parents were putty much absent, leaving the household to Antoinette. She was adorable, taking care of four boys, the apartment, the household.

I got my diploma and my license at the end of my last school year. I was thrilled! We still had a national contest, which I didn't want to miss. That year, in 1959, I was given the best apprenticeship award. I was excited. It was a challenge to test my knowledge and abilities to create, and be judged. I brought a model, performed for forty-five minutes, and then waited. I won third prize. I was disappointed. I promised myself I'd be number one for the next one, and it happened to be in 1960.

We had to come up with a daytime hairdo in forty-five minutes. When performing I was working on air, self-centered among all the contestants, it was eerie. I brushed, teased, and laid down each piece of hair, smoothing each strand with a hairpin. The bell rung and I waited. When my name came up, I couldn't believe it! I was number one! I made my way to the podium to get my diploma, my heartbeat resonating loudly in my chest. Jacques was in the audience, I was in heaven, and in love. I came home with a great piece of paper!

I still hung with my buddies. My next step was to find a job, earn my own money, and take care of my everyday needs. Jacques B. approached me, asking if JJ was going to pick me up that day. Jacques B. invited me for dinner, and we had a lovely evening, laughing, trying new dishes. I was relaxed, having a good time. Suddenly, his black eyes became deep, he took my hand into his, tightly, his face overrun with great emotion. He whispered, "I took a job far away on an island." He liked the deal; it was very promising. But he wanted to take me with him, to be his bride, bear his children. He was in love with me and wanted to build a life together. The ceiling was falling on my head. He was my best friend, and I could trust him in any situation. But what about Jacques? No, I couldn't! As a friend, I told him my dilemma, my choice. His face became bare, emotionless, and then a great sadness took over. We got up from the table, paid the bill, and stood outside. He wrapped his long arms around me, hugging me tightly. It was comfortable, and I felt warm, secure. My head lay on his broad chest, and I just closed my eyes in this special moment. He tenderly kissed my forehead, and then I departed. He remained at the same spot, watching me disappear in the moving crowd.

Rosine, Laurent, Jacques, and I loved to dance and were very good. Jacques and I even won a prize for Best Dancers. We hopped from nightclubs, to discos, swirling all night to Elvis Presley love songs, hugging, kissing, our bodies so close moving in harmony to "Only You" by Sidney Bechet. Jacques and I were at our best. We spent the night dancing, slows, rock and roll, tangos. We belonged to each other, complementing each move, each turn. He was there to catch me. We were a team, burning our energy, having fun.

I went home after my last year of school. After two abortions, one known by Jacques' parents, Jacques surprised me and came to Alsace for my eighteenth birthday. My parents didn't know what to think of him. They were reluctant to receive him but didn't turn him down. He spent the night at home, on a different floor than me. I snuck in his bedroom at night, and we spent an hour together. Nothing was going to get in our way.

A few months later, I noticed few changes within my body. I was nauseous. I was ignorant and didn't know how to protect myself from pregnancy. I couldn't ask anybody! I knew too well what it meant. This time I was going to fight for my baby; I was ready to keep it. I was eighteen and had a professional license. Jacques informed his parents, and his mother made the trip to Cernay, Alsace, to discuss my future. It was on a Sunday. Father was always on time, but this time he came late, probably didn't want to deal with it. I was annoyed but stayed quiet. I will never know what happened, what was said. Father was opposed to the new state of my life, his plans were falling apart, and his ego was hurt. He was ashamed of his daughter. I didn't go through the conventional ways of starting a family; I was his biggest disappointment. Under the stoop of the house, on my way back to Paris, he said, "Don't ever come back." I looked at him and left. Jacques' mother took me to her obstetrician who confirmed my pregnancy and told me I had two solutions: an abortion or keep the baby. If I kept it, the doctor would find a home for my child. I listened, then loudly objected to their solutions. On the defensive I threatened them to contact the authorities if they touched me. Jacques' mother remained stoic. We left the doctor's office without exchanging a word.

Jacques and I were genuinely happy about our reality. We went to see *Orfeo Negro*, a great love story, which reinforced our feelings for each other. On June 11, 1960, we got married! It was a civil marriage at the seventh arrondissement courthouse. Later on we had a reception at his grandparents' apartment; they lived on the other side of the Champs de Mars in a huge apartment with a balcony and large windows. It was the first time I had gone through these beautiful, heavy doors! I took Jacques' arm and held it tight; I didn't know what to expect. I knew this was a new world for me. There were waiters with white gloves in uniform smiling. I wore a two-piece suit made out of white lace from Alencon. Jacques' mother's parents were the owners of this magnificent place. I was introduced to them, and his grandfather welcomed us. He performed a very small ceremony. He sat in his arm chair, took our left hands, put a gold band on our fingers, and pronounced us husband and wife. It was my day! Now I knew I was always going to be with Jacques. Carrying his child was the summit of our love. I mingled with the crowd, knowing only Jacques. I had only met his brothers and his friends twice, so I remained kind of by myself. But I noticed a young lady, dressed in white, going around happily talking to Jacques, touching his arm. I wondered why she was in white; it was *my* day! I brushed away all the unwanted thoughts.

The following week my parents-in-law took me to a place I believe was a lawyer's office. Under the roof of a building along the river Seine, an old Jewish man with a very long, white beard greeted us in a room piled with many, many books and papers everywhere. He presented me with some forms to sign; it was a prenuptial contract. There was no comment from me. I signed. I was too naïve. But I knew I didn't marry Jacques for his money. I didn't even know if he had any! I was going to make my own because I never relied on anybody. Money was not my thing, but right now I wasn't earning any.

I was starting to show, and Jacques' parents put us in a one-bedroom, furnished apartment in Levallois, a suburb northwest of Paris. It was on the first floor, dark, old, and smelly. I didn't mind though because we had a place to build our lives. I arranged it the best I could with very limited means. I made it cheerful. I found a long-haired orange cat to keep me company; I named him Sylvester. I never saw my family, knowing that Father had meant what he said. I didn't stay in touch with Tonton either. I felt very badly about that. I tried to concentrate on my new, strange life. If I was in trouble, I had to solve it on my own.

I felt my baby move inside me. What a feeling! How rewarding it was for me. My breasts were full and painful, though I felt very good. I gained very little weight. Jacques' family had a routine. Every Sunday morning we gathered at 10:30 at his parents' house, then walked to the grandparents' house. Before leaving, an hour later, each of us got some money. This happened every week. It was kind of nice. I was not making any money, and I had to buy things for the baby. His parents took care of the rent plus the utilities. On weekends, Jacques went with his friends after lunch at his parents' house, after dropping me off back home. Routine. I stayed home, prepared meals, washed, ironed, just being a housewife. Jacques was his mother's favorite child. He even looked like her. He never went to school because he didn't like it; therefore, he was homeschooled. Professors came to their home to teach him. His charm was overwhelming, and everybody fell under his spell. He was the spitting image of Alain Delon, a famous, young French actor.

His father was very strict. We always had to be nicely dressed, put together. He would often remind Jacques to get his hair cut. Jean-Pierre, the eldest, was his dad's favorite. Jean-Pierre was strict, articulate, highly educated, cold, distant, and observing; he scared me. I didn't know how to deal with him, so I stayed quiet. I knew I was unwelcome. Michel was a painter, producing no income, so his parents would support him. But he had to endure his father's sarcastic comments. He was one or two years older than Jacques.

Most of the time, Jacques and I were together. After the wedding, I never saw Jacques' friends; they despised pregnant women. Michel had a girlfriend, Armande. She was very sweet, adored Michel, but she wasn't too smart or responsible. But they were love birds. We all went to the movies together, shared meals, and spent evenings listening to music. Every Sunday we were at the parents' and grandparents' house, Armande included.

I was getting bigger and showing more, but my body remained skinny. Jacques didn't like my new look, and our relationship started to change. Little by little we spent less time together. Jacques went with his friends after lunch on Sunday's. On week days he was tired and often brought work home. I wanted to learn so I could help him. That summer we went to his parents' summer house in Cap Ferret near Arcachon. They had it built. It was a contemporary place with very high ceilings, skylights, spacy, and airy. I seldom went to the beach during those years. You just didn't see pregnant women along the shore in those days! I was bored and didn't feel comfortable. I wasn't in my element and nobody really liked me. I couldn't wait to go home to my own world.

On Yom Kippur, we all gathered at the parents' house to celebrate at sundown. In the morning we went to Salle Pleyel, a theater where only classical music was played. Each year it was used on that day to celebrate the Jewish holiday, to listen to a service. We were in the first row, in the middle, in the balcony. I was fascinated, curious. I couldn't follow it, not knowing Hebrew, but seeing the rabbi and the Torah, I wanted to know more about it! It was amazing to see all these people, who were persecuted by an evil man, to be together, celebrating their holiday. After the service we went downstairs. In each room there were different ceremonies taking place, in their native tongues, from all over the world. All celebrating Yom Kippur. It was very impressive.

Afterward we went to his parents' home to celebrate. Antoinette had prepared a special meal, and it was the only time in the year my mother-in-law would prepare one dish, chopped liver, which I adored. I knew I was going to give birth at the end of October, and the time was coming close. I started to prepare my nest: bassinet, diapers enough for two days, little brassiere. I wished I could call my parents, ask for advice and money. I knew Jacques wasn't giving me all his paycheck; he needed money to keep up with his friends. I managed. I was not demanding. When the time came closer, I was a little scared. I missed my mother! And my aunt Tata. One day, very early in the morning, I started to have some contractions. I waited until they came closer, woke up Jacques, and we took a cab to the hospital, Baudelocque. I waited for some time before a doctor came and checked me. He told me to go home, I wasn't ready. Jacques was upset because it had interfered with his schedule. I was in his way. I felt lonely and hurt. Back home I went to bed and tried to sleep. When I woke up the apartment was still. My cat Sylvester was near me, watching me. Jacques was gone, and my contractions came back. I started to do the Lamaze breathing technique and it helped. I waited a little longer, and then took a cab back to Baudelocque. When I stepped in the lobby of the hospital a nurse took care of me, checked me, comforted me, and praised me for being so brave. I knew she felt for me, so young, alone.

After several long hours, I gave birth to a beautiful little boy. He was screaming, exercising his lungs to full capacity. I thought he looked like my father. I had strange feelings since I hadn't seen nor talked to my parents for four months. The nurse gently wiped his body and placed him in my arms. I couldn't believe I made this precious baby, little toes, fingers, so perfect. I was in awe! I enjoyed seeing my son, this wonder. I felt blessed but very isolated. I was in a room with two new mothers, their husbands, and family coming, loving their new addition. I was by myself. I couldn't stop the tear that rolled down my cheek. I looked at my son with a smile on my face, and said, "It's going to be all right!"

My mother-in-law came the next day, took a look at the bassinet, asked me if everything was fine, and left. I was in the hospital for a week — the required time — and Jacques had only come to see me once when he glimpsed at the baby and then left. When my son was born, the nurses asked me if I wanted the baby to be circumcised. I had said no. I remembered the young man shot in front of me by a German soldier. I was very happy to have my child, but something wasn't right; I could feel it! Again I brushed it away, dealing with each day, adapting to my new situation.

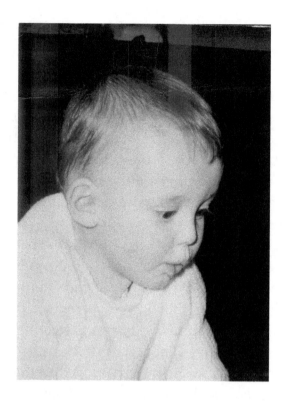

Jacques came to pick us up to bring us home. To my great surprise we stopped at his grandparents' house; his parents were there also. On a very long dining room table was a very large, fluffy white pillow. Our son was gently placed on it, undressed. At my astonishment, they checked him out and were relieved he had passed the test. He was a beautiful baby, and I was very proud. We named him Laurent after Jacques' best friend. I was in a hurry to go home to put the little one in his bassinet, feed him, and change him. Jacques didn't know what to do! It wasn't part of his way of life. Sylvester was gone, to my great disarray. I will never know what happened to my beautiful, loving cat.

I programmed my day, taking care of Laurent, the apartment, and making meals. Every Sunday, when we went to see his grandparents, we now spent up to three hours, rather than the normal one hour. Our place was really dark. No matter how I perked it up it wasn't a young couple's place. My mother-in-law would come without warning, overlooking things!

Laurent became a baby with a lot of personality, always smiling, busy, and happy. During one visit to the grandparents' house, when news came up about the past, especially the war, they would speak about their fear, their hiding. One day his grandmother had a premonition to not go to the synagogue, so they stayed put. She was right. That day the Germans raided the place! My father-in-law was a Freemason — an elite, influential group discussing politics and news. Each member had a number and went by it; it was their identity. During their meeting they knew the German Army positions and their goals, so he sent his family to the southern part of France, where they were protected. He was taken by the Germans and sent to a concentration camp. There they realized he spoke six languages, so they used him as a translator, fortunately for him. Though it was tough, witnessing tortures and seeing masses going to the chambers. These real stories always left me wondering how evil people could be, what kind of satisfaction they could have physically and mentally. It also made me think about the will of people to live, to endure the inhumane, unbelievable suffering. I never spoke about my own bout with the war buried deep within me and the consequences from it, like fear, claustrophobia, and sleeping with a mouchi, as I still do.

Jacques' parents decided to buy us a condo south of Paris, Montrouge, a nice suburb. It was a one bedroom one bath in a new development. I was ready to be in a sunny, joyful place with lots of windows. I chose the bare minimum to furnish it — a bed, a table with four chairs, a chest. His parents gave us a library, a drawing table, and high chair for Jacques' work. I kept in touch with Tata who bought us a place setting for eight; I was set. Jacques brought his friends here. I sort of knew he never left "The Group," but I was longing for a family life. I could see my wish slipping. My father-in-law had warned me that Jacques wasn't mature. Now I had the urge to make my own money, knowing deeply I wasn't going to stay in this situation. I wanted to be independent, take the rein.

I inquired about a daily nanny in the complex and found a young lady with a four-year-old son. We liked each other, so the deal was made. From Tuesday to Saturday she would take care of Laurent. I went back to my school to look for a job. There were many diverse offers. I chose a shop, Rue Saint-Denis, where prostitutes made their business. They would have their hair done every day, which was a learning experience for me as well as lucrative. I was set to change the course of my life.

On my way to the metro, one of the teachers stopped his car and asked me if I wanted a ride. His home was in Montrouge where I lived, so I agreed and hopped in his car. We were talking, and I was not paying attention to where we were going. I suddenly found myself in front of the door of an elevator from the street. He lured me upstairs. I was stunned to find myself in a bedroom facing a man who had become aggressive, animal-like, ready to jump on me. I knew I had a challenge! There was nowhere to go. I ran around the room and he grabbed me. I tried to escape his grip, my heart pounding. He ripped my silk blouse apart, and I pulled the pieces over my bra, still trying to avoid him. Finally he got me, his face full of grim of desire, wild, his eyes ready to jump out of their sockets, his hands all over me. The bed showed my struggle, my fight. There was blood everywhere. Meanwhile, he became more and more frustrated and angry. My teacher and I left the room, and I tried to cover myself. I had no feelings, just overwhelmed by a great disgust for men. My teacher dropped me in front of our apartment without saying a word. I ran inside and took a shower before going to pick up Laurent. I was hurt, sad, and blamed myself for trusting people, for getting in this situation. However, life went on as usual.

The incident made me realize my marriage had not been consummated. We lived under the same roof, spent less and less time together, and he always went back to The Group he had never left. My priority was to have a job to take care of the nanny and my expenses. So I took a job on Rue Saint Denis. It was a small shop, which I liked. It was friendly and I felt good. Soon we became very busy. They called me Nefertiti. I was energetic and had a goal. I became very well-known on the block. People flocked there to see me. By this time, I had had a lot of practice and became very good, fast, confident, and self-assured. I had an education, I behaved better than my peers, people respected me, and told me I was beautiful.

One day when I was heading to the metro from work, a gentleman stalked me. A prostitute came to my rescue, told him off, and walked with me. I felt protected and loved, something that was missing at home. The situation became worse. We didn't communicate anymore; we rode on different waves. One Saturday I got a phone call from Jacques at the shop, asking me if I was going to our friends' party. I said I didn't know when my day was going to end. After work, I went home, picked up Laurent, put him in his

crib, called a cab, and showed up at the gathering. A test!
When I rang the bell I heard Jacques shouting, "My wife!"
I sort of knew what I was going to discover. Everybody
looked at me strangely, even though we were buddies. I knew
something was brewing. The host was the same woman who
came to my wedding dressed in white. I had the feeling, and
somehow knew they had been together. I went to the buffet
like nothing happened, made small talk with his not-so-
friendly friends, and then Jacques asked me about Laurent.
I told him he was home in his bassinet. He was upset,
drove me home, dumped me in front of the apartment, and
went back to the party. I was very hurt. My castle had just
crumbled. The parents on both sides were right; I was just
too stubborn and too much in love. And now I was being
tested! How long could I carry on? I took my child close
to my heart and closed my eyes; he was the only thing I
cared for. I had to fight, love him, and raise him. It was my
commitment to somebody I brought into this world.

One Sunday at his parents home, Laurent took his first
steps, and he wasn't even a year old yet! Everybody was in
awe. He was such a charming, loving child. Jacques' friend,

a photographer for a very well-known company, took pictures of Laurent. A few months later I got a phone call from an agency wanting Laurent to be Bebe Cadum, an advertisement for baby's soap. I turned it down. I didn't want my child to be in every metro station, on buses, to be bait for kidnapping. No. At work, they now compared me to Grace Kelly and Catherine Deneuve. Nice to hear. I was so lonely, not loved, living in a sterile home. The only joy was Laurent's smile. At the parents' gathering, my mother-in-law told me I should wear my skirts longer, now that I was a mother. Then she asked me if we had enough money to cover our expenses. I always said yes, and then Jacques would say we went to the theater, to the movies, and other leisure things, so she would give him more. I was appalled how he could lie to his mother like that, but that was Jacques! He started also to gamble and play poker like his mother. He became very, very good and won quite a bit. My work became my focus. I was doing very well and loved by my clients. The shop owners all around knew me, protected me, and helped me. I didn't want to admit my marriage was falling apart because I was a fighter. I wanted to stay in it for my son, so I waited until I couldn't take it anymore.

One Monday the photographer came by to see us when Jacques wasn't there. He came to tell us he had been drafted to do his military duty. He was leaving in few days. We had some wine, and the conversation drifted to my personal life. He knew my dilemma, my unhappiness. He felt sorry for me, probably knowing more than me about Jacques' escapades! I was sinking under my problems. He took me in his arms and I melted. I gave in, and my loneliness and unhappiness vanished. I hadn't felt a body for months. His hands contoured my body and I trembled. We kissed passionately, rolling on the floor, our legs intertwined, feeling his chest hair on my chest. We lay there, panting. It felt so good I was in awe.

Finally I got a call from Father asking me to come home and visit them. Laurent and I went by train, in the sleeping section, an eight-hour ride. Father was at the station to pick us up. He was surprised to see Laurent so grown up — of course he had never seen him. We had a lovely evening talking and getting reacquainted with each other. The next morning I put Laurent on the potty, and my father came to me telling me something was wrong. Laurent couldn't hold his head up and he was red. Father panicked and called our family physician, who called the ambulance.

I didn't hear anything for three days. Finally they told me he had meningitis. Father brought me to see him. He was in a huge room with many beds and children wearing the same gowns. I went row by row when a little voice said, "Mama!" I had passed him. I turned and he was there, smiling, his arms out to me. What a relief! To hear my son calling me was a blessing because I knew that meningitis could be life threatening. I hugged him tightly, my most precious belonging. I wanted to take him home right then, but he had to stay another week. So I went back to Paris, and then came back to get him. My parents knew things weren't right, but they didn't mention anything, just hugged me tightly. Father said the door would always be open! It warmed my heart; I needed it.

My clients became my family. Sometimes they brought me flowers or treated me for lunch. My days were packed. I made a lot of money, but I had a lot of expenses, and Jacques was contributing less and less. My life was in shambles. I was still fighting to stay in the marriage for my son's sake. My place, I loved so much, became a witness of a failed marriage. I received some mail from the photographer who missed me, loved me, and couldn't wait to come back to be with me. I was flattered but I didn't love him and didn't see spending my life with him. He was very talented and had a great future in front of him, but it wasn't for me.

Laurent and I were making the best of it. We never knew when Jacques would come home. We were going in different directions, sliding away from each other without end. Sometimes The Group would come on Saturdays when I was at work, so one of these Saturdays I opened the door and noticed spaghetti hanging from the ceiling, the sink in the bathroom, and on the floor. I was outraged! If he wanted to destroy his property, fine, but I was still living there! I had to find a plumber and pay for repairs with my own money.

At work I met Yvette, a client, who worked in the fashion district not far from the shop. I was attracted to her for her wisdom, advice, serenity, and stability, which I was lacking. I met another wonderful lady, Brigitte, a mother of two girls, who was divorced from a surgeon. She kind of took me under her wing. I liked her very much as a best friend, a mother, and a big sister; she was 10 years older. We had a lot in common. When things had gotten worse for me, she invited me to stay in her home.

On my way home I wondered, *How long can I take my disintegrating life?* I arrived at my apartment to find Jacques with a lady in our bed. They both looked at me in either disbelief or embarrassment. I told them to get out, and Jacques and his lady got dressed and left. The next day Jacques came to pick up Laurent and me to go to his parents' house. I was quieter than usual, pondering what I was going to do, unable to explain our situation. After a sharp question from his father, leaving me speechless, I got up, took my son and my purse under my arm, and left without saying a word. I couldn't explain to them what was going on; they wouldn't have believed me. I was always an outsider and never felt comfortable. It was the last time I put my feet on Av. General Trippier. This was my last week at our apartment. I needed to find a nanny!

Somebody at work recommended a young lady, divorced, who kept children. She lived in the suburbs, Asniere, in a high-rise. She was nice and clean. I had to take a train, and then walk for twenty minutes to reach her house. It wasn't ideal, but for the time being, it would have to work. He stayed there all week, and then I picked him up every Saturday. During that week, after coming home, I found my mother-in-law in my apartment. She waved some letters in front of my face threatening me, blaming me for her beloved son's misfortune and then left, content. She had proof to nail me. Those papers were love letters from the photographer. I packed Laurent's clothes, mine, and moved out to Pigalle's apartment. It was very difficult to make these decisions. I was twenty, had a two-year-old son, a good job, and a roof. I felt like a drifter. Work was tumultuous also.

One of the owners was after me; he knew my status. I was a little older than his daughter, who looked up to me. I was cornered so I took a week off. Laurent and I went to Trouville, a well-known resort. I rented a room in a hotel not far from the beach. It was sunny and warm, a different environment that was good for both of us. Every morning at breakfast we would see this good-looking, mature man dressed in a suit. Our gaze would lock with intensity. Laurent couldn't stay still. He wandered from table to table, talking to everybody, but he always stopped at this gentleman's table.

He would sit and have a conversation. Everybody knew Laurent! On the boardwalk he made friends, posing in front of the photographer, jumping. He was a natural-born actor.

After few days the gentleman came to my reserved table, introduced himself, and started a conversation, at my son's delight. I didn't know anything about him, except his name was Richard. We spoke of opera, which he loved! It was the first time somebody shared my likes; as a hobby he was a tenor. He came to see us in my room to say hello. I had some classical music on, and he started to sing. His deep, strong, vibrant voice reached higher notes; I was in awe! I thought I may be standing next to an opera singer! It left me helpless, taking everything in, his talent overwhelming me.

A few days later Laurent and I had to go back to Paris, so Richard and I exchanged telephone numbers. I was happy! It was the first time I had met a man I truly liked, whom I could express myself with, and have a mature conversation about arts, opera. We went back home, Laurent to his nanny and me to Brigitte. Laurent was a fascinating little child who was into everything and interested in anything. I was proud of him. One weekend, with a group of friends, we went to Montmartre, Place du Tertre, where artists practiced their talents. One called me and wanted to do my portrait. When he finished, he proudly put it in front of me with a big smile, waiting for my approval. I nodded. Yes, it was me! I put it on top of my chest in my room.

Brigitte spent her weekends on the racetracks, dragging me, her children. I was fascinated to see these beautiful, groomed, handsome horses. She was involved with a horse trainer so she had free tickets. Of course she also gambled. It was exciting to see these perfect creatures racing, running, their hooves barely touching the ground, winning or losing.

I became quite involved in the process, checking to see if the horses perspired, were nervous, their attitudes, the jockeys. I learned it was not just betting; it was also the atmosphere.

We went to the Grand Prix de Paris in Longchamps, then we visited the racetracks at Bois de Vincennes, St. Cloud, Auteuil. I was really into it. Colorful, exciting, a lot of movement, life, nice people, well dressed. It was the type of crowd I liked. One day I got a call from Richard. He wanted me to meet him in Evreux, a city between Paris and Trouville. I took the train, so excited, and couldn't wait to see him, to be hugged, to be loved, to get back those magic moments when we met. I couldn't believe he was in front of me, this enigmatic man I didn't know anything about, yet I was drawn toward him. We had a fantastic time, we held hands, and it felt good. I learned he was a bank manager in Trouville who was connected to the casinos. I felt loved for who I was. We discussed very little about our personal lives; instead, we directed our thoughts toward opera and our feelings for the singers. It was the first time I was in peace, content. I idealized him in my state of mind; he was my remedy for the time being. He was strong, forward, no game, no lies. However, my feelings were platonic; we never had physical relations. He always kissed me on my cheeks or forehead. I wrote him romantic letters, passionate, about a better future. Sometimes when I was down, my writings showed disbelief in life, in men. I read a lot of books by Joseph Kessel, Maurice Druon, Henry Troyat, John Knittel, Guy des Cars, and John Steinbeck. It was my escape. Going to movies strengthened my way of thinking; there must be happiness. Richard brought me stability. I got a call one day that he was coming to Paris for a meeting and that we should meet. I was looking forward to seeing him again, to being hugged, feeling his arms, his chest. During lunch, I was bubbling with excitement and he was quiet, listening, watching me. I gave him the portrait drawn by the painter. He said, "You are beautiful." I acknowledged, smiled. While we were walking, he abruptly stopped, put his arms on my shoulders, and our eyes locked. He said, "This is the last time I am going to see you. I am married, not happily, but I have an autistic son. He had a seizure yesterday, and my duty is to take care of him." I looked at him, my eyes widening in disbelief. He took his hands off me and handed me my portrait.

I said, "No, it is for you."

He nodded, kissed my cheeks, and left. My dream was vanishing. I went back to my world. I understood. He was getting attached. I was his escape; I represented what he loved, youth, freshness, without attachments. I was eager to learn, to discover. I made his life interesting.

A few weeks later I got a phone call from a movie producer asking me if I would let Laurent play a piece in a movie he was making. He had seen his picture in a studio at the Champs Elysee, where my friend worked. Again, I denied the offer. A short time later, Jacques advised me that his parents hired a lawyer. I couldn't face another hurdle. At work one client, Pierrot, came frequently, to chat with the owner or to have something done. He laid his eyes on me, and each time he came he would call me, asking me what I was doing. I was always vague but polite. Although sunburned, he was always groomed, wore a lot of jewelry, and had a beautiful smile. One day he asked me out for a lunch date, to Place de l'Opera. That day it was raining hard and I decided not to go. Anyway, he scared me. I had never been close to a black person before, and I felt I wouldn't know how to act. The next day Interpol stormed in the shop asking for me. We went to the cafe next door to talk, and they showered me with questions. They asked me, "Why didn't you go on your date!" I got scared! Why were they asking me all these questions? How did they know about my date with Pierrot? Turns out, he was being investigated for recruiting young ladies to be sent to Africa. They said, "He was part of an organization for white slavery, human trafficking. These women would never see freedom again because we'd lose their trace. You were our bait!" I was perplexed, my instinct had protected me. I escaped a horrible future, and I was glad I followed my guts. I didn't peep a word of this to anybody. I concentrated my thoughts on my clients and the prostitutes, from whom I learned a lot, like how they got involved in the business. Some used to be teachers, nurses, and students. They never could get out of it because they were either blackmailed or threatened. They taught me how to protect myself — never accept a date or a drink with a man I didn't know! Once you accepted you were hooked, and there was no way out. These ladies had such big hearts, even with their lousy lives.

One day one of my clients asked me if I wanted to make quick, fast money. I asked her, "How!"

"You come with me to Marseille and you stand on the corner; you don't have to do too much."

I said, "No, it's not for me." She understood my reasoning and remained my client.

A stunning young lady came to my shop several times, and we became acquainted. Two weeks later she came back, and she had lost so much weight! She looked haggard, lost. My heart fell! What happened? She barely could walk. I was curious. She was slurring, incoherent, shaking, and said she needed something. She was hooked on opium, lying on bamboo mats in a basement somewhere all alone. I would never forget this. In the future whenever I encountered drugs, I remembered the destruction, the cause of her death, her picture coming to my mind, and how she needed help. How dreadful to lose life this way!

Then I met another lady with the most beautiful light green eyes, like the river Nile. She was pleasant, always smiling, put together. She always came with two men who catered to her, pampering her. I was puzzled. During a deep conversation about relationships, she told me that her husband had become impotent, so she brought in a lover and the threesome lived together, happily. It was the best of both worlds. They treated each other with respect and dignity. I was impressed.

After Richard went out of my life, things started to get worse. I was very comfortable at Brigitte's. I had nice meals and a beautiful setting, but it was time for me to move on; they had their own lives. I was very appreciative of their hospitality. I moved to a small room in a hotel on the left bank. I spent most of the time at work anyway. I would have a hot meal at the cafe, then after work I would buy a baguette and some jambon de Paris — my favorite, only in Paris could I find that kind — and a piece of Swiss cheese. I would have Laurent on weekends. I was homesick and needed a change of scenery, so Laurent and I went home for a few days.

Saturday night I went dancing at the Griffon, a bar with a dance floor, where people of all ages gathered. It was well known, and they always had a great band. I danced all night with a tall, blond young man with blue eyes. We were a great couple, swinging in harmony, dancing the night away, laughing. He was puzzled by my looks, my way of conducting a discussion, my manners. I was very different from all the women he had ever met before. We liked each other and made a good match; it was what I needed, rejuvenation, to be myself. He drove me home, a short distance, and we exchanged phone numbers.

The next day he called, inviting me to go to Basel. We drove in his Mercedes to Basel and strolled the city. In late afternoon we went to a fancy first-class restaurant where the waiters wore starched white shirts, white gloves, and served us flambé lobster in a cognac sauce with sautéed bananas. Then we went to a nightclub with a striptease on stage, done slowly with class, teasing our curiosity. Drinks were served at our table. It was a memorable, smooth, classy evening among the rich and famous.

The next day he came to pick me up again. We drove to the beautiful city of Geneva for lunch. We went to a restaurant on a boat on Lake Leman. It was elegant with only the top clientele. There I discovered the finest dish: Loup de Mer, a Mediterranean fish. It melted in my mouth with a taste of anise. To be among beautiful, elegant, well-mannered people, and the luxury of the boat, transported me to an unreachable world. I took it all in with delight. I learned that he had a chain of cleaners in Mulhouse where he lived. We had a great time together. If I had moved back home, my life would have turned out much differently. He drove me back to my parents' house early in the morning. It was a lovely experience. Now that my stay in Alsace was over, it was back to the jungle.

At work I became very close to Yvette, who was few years older. She lived with her family, consisting of three sisters and a mother, which she became for me also. Later on, they rented a huge apartment near Madeleine, furnished with antiques, beautiful paintings, and a long dining room table. We all talked, laughed, and enjoyed the happy environment. Her mother was small, energetic, and a master in the kitchen. They used nice china, silver, crystal, and a huge bouquet of magnificent flowers were always on display.

The Kouyoumdjians had settled in the southern part of France, having fled the Armenian revolution. Mr. Kouyoumdjian, a biologist, practiced his experiments in a small detached house on the property. One day everything caught on fire, with him in it! So the family moved to Paris, where they could find work and build from there. When I met them they had a small business making clothes, selling them to boutiques and having fashion shows. Mini was the eldest, an administrator, accountant. Annie was the designer. Yvette did a little of everything: sewing, cutting, choosing fabrics. Monique had a mental problem, so she was close to her mother; it was a family affair. Mini was gregarious with a deep, commanding, raspy voice and sharp eyes. She was the controller in the family. She had class; you couldn't miss her. Her husband, Turk, owned a jewelry store in Deauville and played bridge with my mother-in-law. Annie was the model of her designs. She was very exotic looking: tall, thin, darker skin color, a mane of thick black hair, dark almond-shaped eyes that were almost impenetrable, a deep voice. She had a son and a husband named Andre. Yvette was very light skinned with thick black hair, and beautiful green eyes. She was the head of the seamstresses; she chose the materials. The mother stayed in the background, helping. They were a very productive, happy family.

At work it wasn't so friendly anymore. The owner, who was after me, finally got to me; we had an affair. Then he

wanted to rule me. Out of rebellion, I had a date with
a friend of his who lived in South Africa, Agadir. I was
tempted to move there, away from the mess. I wasn't happy
with Laurent's arrangement either; it was too far and the
environment didn't suit me. I wasn't ready yet to make the
move. I became Marcel's toy. Several times in the week, after
work, we would meet in the same hotel room. I knew there
was no love, an attraction. One day, a woman came in the
room to join us. I was surprised and then revolted. That was
the end of our relationship. I have to say, Marcel taught me a
lot about how to become a partner, to enjoy the senses God
gave us, to enjoy each other in an effort to reach a climax.
I realized I really was a thing to play with, trying anything,
everything.

I became friendly with the cleaner's manager, Renee. She
was always happy and came by to see me every day. She lived
around the corner with her husband, very somber, shy. One
Monday, she invited me to have lunch at their apartment. I
was happy to go, to get out of my hotel room. I brought a
dozen roses. When I arrived her husband opened the door
and then locked it behind me. I gave him the roses, sat on
the sofa, and tried to have a conversation. After some time,
I asked about Renee. He told me that she had gone to see
their son in the country. So then what was I doing there!
He became agitated, trying to grab me! I thought, *Here we
go again*. The vision with the teacher came to my mind. It
was the same situation. I ran around the table and chairs,
and after a short time he grabbed my top, threw me on the
sofa, and jumped on top of me. He slapped me, my head
tilting from one side to the other. I fought back and lost a
nail in the process. He was fueled with envy, desire, his eyes
devilish. Thank God the clothes saved me. The skirt was so

narrow he couldn't push it up! So after fighting and wrestling he stopped and gave up, frustrated, annoyed. He took the roses, threw them down the stairs, and that was the end of my friendship with Renee and the beginning of my will to change the course of my life.

I encountered an Algerian man who acknowledged me; he looked like the one who followed me in Alsace. The one who sat for three days in front of my parents house. I was scared then and wouldn't tell my parents. It was so strange to see him in Paris and in the area I was in. Creepy! A shiver went down my spine, remembering my fears.

I loved my clients. They came to me — besides my cosmetology skills — to find comfort. For them it was a serene place where they could talk, find affection, friendship. Meanwhile, Jacques wanted to see me, so we met. My heart pounded and my legs shook. He asked me to come back! I looked at him surprised. How could he ask me this? After all he did, crushing my feeling, my first and only love, my identity, reducing me to nothing! Inside I still loved him; he was so charming, gregarious. I fell for it so many times. No, nothing would change. It was time to make a stop and show him who I was.

I met another young man, Yves, who was different from anybody I knew. He was gentle, soft, and infatuated with me. By that time I was desperate to find love! So I gave it a try. I knew I had to get out of the circle I was revolving in; it wasn't healthy. I gave him a chance, though, inside of me I kind of knew it wasn't going to work out physically, intellectually. I brushed my thought away. We moved into a furnished, one-bedroom apartment together, an impressive building on Av. de la Grande Armee. Our furniture was antique, and we had beautiful paintings, Chinese trinkets

. . . it was cozy. Things were smooth at the beginning. He was very attentive to Laurent, going out of his way to please us. Each time I would open a drawer, or a closet, I would find a love note, some love verses. At the beginning, it was amusing, and then it became annoying. As the days went by, I knew I had made another mistake. Jacques came to return Laurent one afternoon in front of the building. He was impressed by the location and the structure, but he didn't know what was happening behind the doors. Yves became very possessive, and I became impatient, edgy, and crushed by never-ending questions. I was like a butterfly; I needed space, trust, freedom, and no walls. I knew where my boundaries were. Another hurdle was that Yves had lost his job and couldn't find another one. So he sat at home and it was eating him up, making him depressed.

One day when I came home from work, the apartment door was open. I pushed it and saw the police investigating! What? They questioned me about my whereabouts. Yves had been taken by ambulance to the American Hospital nearby. He had slashed his wrists! A fury invaded my mind. I became angry, frustrated by all my misfortune created by my stupidity. I analyzed my state of mind. I should stick to my goals, forget about my loneliness, my desire of being a couple, and start over to keep my sanity. My divorce was almost done; a police report would change everything! When I went to the hospital, he looked at me with so much love and said, "I am sorry." I was outraged, overwhelmed by negative thoughts. He didn't work and lived on my earnings. Why was I attracting these kinds of people? I knew I was on the wrong track. I needed to change, get out of the negative, destructive circle I was in. Yves was a nice man but not for me. I told him I was leaving him.

There was a difference between city and country people, which I noticed between my father and Tonton. People in a big city stuck together, race-wise. Then there were the pimps and the prostitutes, the drugs dealers and the distributors, the lower, middle, upper class . . . nobody mixed, except to make a deal or a transaction. You had to climb the ladder and your past was your shadow; it never left you. In a small town, everybody knew anyone, your moves, your status, your wealth.

I returned to my best friends, the Kouyoumdjian family, where I got true, genuine love. I went back to school to see where they needed a hairstylist. I found one in the 15th arr. I went for an interview; a lady in her 30th was the owner. We liked each other and the deal was set. Then I booked a monthly room in a small hotel, not far away. I was excited to start. I introduced myself to the staff, and everything went smoothly.

A week later I belonged to the group; I was accepted as one of them. The other task to resolve was to find a nanny for Laurent. A coworker's mother-in-law took care of children, so I had an interview with Mrs. Parizy, a lady with a lot of wit. When she saw Laurent they hit it off, and Laurent felt comfortable with her. I went to the local school to register my son; the proximity was great. I felt comfortable with the arrangement. As I settled with my coworkers, Yvette came to tell me there was a studio for rent in the complex where Annie and Andre lived on Av. de New York, near the Champs Elysee, an upper-class district. I agreed. It was a new beginning. This time, I knew it was a good, clean environment. Annie and Andre were close by. If I needed anything they were there. They often invited me over for a drink or a meal, wrapping me with love, friendship, taking me the way I was. I could grow, develop, and mature. We went to the movies and listened to music. When we could get tickets we went to the operetta at the Chatelet, another beautiful theater. It was a remarkable move; I was very happy. The streets were crowded night and day with all kinds of people. At her mother's place, at the Madeleine, we strolled the great store Fauchon, with a delicatessen I had never seen before. I couldn't stop my mouth from watering. The presentation and their artistic ways drew people into the store where they would gladly open their wallets; they mastered the art of of luring consumers. I felt right in my skin, rejuvenated, getting a new start, the right one.

The divorce was now finalized. I kept our son, and let Jacques have him two weekends a month. We shared the cost of the nanny, which was fine with me. On our way out of court, my father-in-law told me, "If you need anything, we will be here." We departed. Jacques and I went to the same metro station but on opposite sides. Our eyes locked, tears rolling down our cheeks. We were twenty-two and twenty-three. The train came and *WWWRRROMMPP* swept me to a new chapter.

I became part of the Kouyoumdjian family and involved in the fashion business. I modeled some clothes for future buyers and choose material with Yvette. I learned there were two collections: one for Europe and one for US. I asked why. In Europe, people were more subdued. Americans liked vibrant colors, though black was a big seller. They introduced me to friends of theirs, also Armenian, who worked with furs. They would choose the pelts and put together a coat, jacket, or vest from a design for Christian Dior's Collection. Then they had another one for different buyers at a lower prize without the label. It was exciting, a new field, a new circle of artists mixed with business people. I learned a lot.

The field was clean, straight, and friendly. The furriers were such nice people; they took me in. One day they presented me with a fur coat to thank me for helping them. It was a black Astrakhan coat, straight collar, very young looking. I loved it! It was warm, cozy, and now I blended in with my surroundings. I started to feel better. My son, my work, my friends . . . everything was in order.

We went out a lot, and one show struck me: the Russian ballet. The strength of the men, the variation of their jumps, their dexterity, the grace of the ballerinas, their mobility, and the music was all very impressive. I had always been inspired by Russian literature, art, and music. Some weekends we would go to the country, the Fontainebleau woods, and stop at a little restaurant. We'd have a great meal on the terrace, taking in the sun, the fresh air, the welcoming breeze playing with our hair. *This* was living! Sometimes we would go to a well-known restaurant on the river, enjoying the nature and the people. So refreshing.

Yvette met a married man who had two children. She dated him for some time and began to loosen up, become more open. The family became concerned about her future, when suddenly they broke it off. Yvette was depressed. To change her state of mind, Annie and Andre planned a trip to Italy, including me. We stopped for lunch in an inviting-looking bistro and spent the night in a cramped hotel room. Yvette put her pants under the mattress to take the creases out. Early we departed for Rome; we all had a bad night. On our way to Pisa, Yvette remembered her pants; she had forgotten to take them out from underneath the mattress. But now it was too late. We arrived at the city of the leaning tower with tourists everywhere. I lost my glasses and Yvette lost her diamond ring after washing her hands.

Other than that, our trip was a delight. We got first-class treatment, but the parking would cost us four times more because of the size of the car. We had never seen so many Vespas and Fiats.

We entered Rome. It was quiet impressive with masses of houses built on a hill, and then a statue of Victor Emanuel greeted us. We strolled the streets of the old city, the multiple boutiques, checking the cashmere sweaters, the silks, the antiques. Then we went to the Vatican, a grandiose complex with many buildings and special guards. We went from street to street admiring everything, until we found a small restaurant with an appealing menu. Our destination, for a month, was Sorrento.

The Tramontano Hotel was built on top of a cliff, and the beach was accessible by an elevator built in the rock. They had a big pool overlooking the sea. Sorrento was known for the best view along the coast, which became famous. It was lovely; we were in a different world. We rented a little Fiat to get around. The streets were hilly and narrow, and we often went to the center of town where there were lots of galleries and antique shops. I bought an oil painting of Capri. In the evenings we would eat at the formal dining room in the hotel; it was good food. There was a man and his mother staying at the hotel; he had eyes on me. One day we bumped into each other, and he asked me to meet him the next day to go sightseeing. He was an Italian banker from Naples and came here to get away. We had a lovely day. He spoke English, and we talked about everything and nothing. I told him I was divorced and had a son. We departed on a very friendly, happy note. The next day he ignored me at the restaurant, and his mother had a disdained look on her face. Being Catholic she disregarded me.

The next day from Naples we took a water plane to bring us to the island of Ischia, which had small, beautiful beaches with white sand. Many houses along the shore and on hills overlooked the magnificent view. After browsing around we had lunch at a terrace, watching people going by, children chasing each other.

The next trip was to Capri. We waited a long time to hop in a barque; there were ten of us with two guides. They paddled us to an opening in a volcanic rock. There was a chain we hung on to and pulled us to the inside. It was very beautiful. A blue glow illuminated the walls of the grotto, hence the name. We didn't stay too long. While departing, the sea became kind of rough, and we were rocking badly. Everybody started to get sick. It was a horrific sight. With our feet on solid ground, we all decided to visit the island, enjoy the breeze, and the walking made us feel better. Going through the narrow streets we wound our way to Ana Capri, a secluded, glamorous gathering of classy estates and influential people living here to relax. Everyone had a pool.

Our next stop was Positano. We drove from one coast to the other. I loved the setup of the town with its small streets. We had lunch in a restaurant built in a rock overlooking the sea. The steps, made in the stone on the verge of the cliff, brought us to the entrance. On each side barbecues sizzled with fish or meat, flavoring the atmosphere with smells. The herbs crackling under the fire made every stomach rumble, every mouth water. We chose a table close to the edge, the view forever etched in our minds.

On our next trip, to Amalfi, charming white houses sat close together and boats docked everywhere. We had one more place to see. Naples.

We were disappointed by the city. We founded it to be dirty, people eating on the sidewalk, skinny, tanned from their hard jobs. Back at the hotel, our last week, we decided to take it easy and exchange our feelings about our trip. It wasn't long before we had to pack, hop in the Skylark, and head back home. We brought with us wonderful memories. They will remain all our lives.

Many months later we still talked about our great Italian stay. We all went back to our respective routines. At work at Denise's salon I had to build up my clientele. I got close to Robert. I was longing for a steady relationship. He was a year older, and we had many things in common. He loved antiques, shows, and he was much more mature than Jacques. So we spent time talking when we were not busy. One of his colleagues moved to Dijon to open his own business, he invited me to go with him for the opening. We arrived in the town, reserved a hotel room, and changed to formal clothes. We looked smashing! Robert was also a very good-looking man. We got to the shop and mingled with people. We drank champagne, ate canapes, and had a good time flirting. On our way to the hotel, we were faced with how to share a room. He helped me take my dress off, his hands barely touching my skin, teasing me. Goose flesh erupted all over my body, I wanted more, to feel his masculinity. It had been a long time since I was close to a man. We kissed, exploring our bodies. We became a couple that night.

On our drive back home we realized we had a lot in common. I was infatuated by his charm, coolness, easy living, though formal when needed. Since we worked at the same salon, we got closer, but in the evenings we would go to our respective homes. Robert was married, had a

daughter, and their relationship was on life support. I was
looking for a small place to rent closer to work. Laurent
was at Mrs. Parizy's, which wasn't too far away. A few streets
from the main avenue, Rue Platon, I found one room with
a window, a kitchen sink, and the bathroom and shower
were the hall! I took it. I moved out of Yvette's place, bought
a small refrigerator, a two-burner gas butane stove, a single
bed that converted to a sofa, and a rug. Robert built me a
three-door closet covered with mirrors, making the room
seem bigger. I had two shelves, the top one for a TV and a
corner shelf between the bed and the closet to put a clock
and telephone on, and a table next to the sink. I was set.
I even had an inflated bed for Laurent. I added a standing
lamp, a housewarming present Robert gave me. I put a small,
bronze antique lamp on the corner shelf as my night light. I
was close to work, Laurent, the metro station, a cafe, some
shops, and a bistro with a reasonable menu. Robert and I
were there often, became acquainted with the owners, and
sometimes, after work, I would stop there on my way home.
I loved the place because it was small and catered to the local
people. They were friendly and they liked me. I would order
a scotch, relax, and Robert would go home to his wife.

One evening a middle-aged man came to sit next to me.
He was very interesting. We ended up discussing opera. He
had tickets to see an opera in Vienna, Austria. I was stunned
to meet somebody who would go that far to see a show,
and so he invited me! I thought, *Why not!* We decided to
leave early Sunday morning; Robert was never with me on
weekends. On Sunday he waited for me in his Mercedes.
I took a bag with me with a change of clothes. When he
greeted me he gave me a present: a beautiful alligator billfold
with a 100fr. I thank him and didn't think anything about it.

On our way to the opera, we stopped at my parents' house.
My father looked at me funny. I explained I was going to see
an opera in Vienna, and my parents were quiet.

We arrived in Vienna before lunch and went to the hotel.
We were hungry so we had lunch. He asked me if I wanted
to take a bath and I said yes. I figured why not, after such
a long ride. So he ran the water in the tub and I got in. He
started to try to wash me, and I told him I didn't need help.
Then when I got out with the towel around me, he grabbed
me and threw me on the bed. I was baffled and thought, *Not
again.* I pushed him away, annoyed, angry. He told me he
had never seen eyes sharper than a sword and he let me go.
We never went to see the opera; instead, we returned home
without saying a word. It was very uncomfortable. I couldn't
wait to be in my little room with people I trusted. Robert
knew about my trip to Vienna, and he didn't like it.

As time went on our relationship became intense. One
day he decided to move in with me. We never spoke about
his past. He was involved in mine because of Laurent, and he
knew my son came first.

Bettina was a colorist. I became very close to her. She was
dating Roland, who also worked with us. Roland idolized
Robert, so we were often together. Robert and Bettina,
excellent cooks, would prepare us a meal that was out of
this world. Robert and I always ate well with these two. We
picnicked and barbecued on weekends. I remembered small
fresh sardines bought at the fish market down the street,
grilled on a small barbecue with fresh herbs . . . it was sooo
good. I never had the pleasure to duplicate this delight.
Robert had built a folding table under the two shelves, so
when we had guests we would pull it out and put a white
tablecloth on it. I managed to have a few Limoges plates,

Saint Louis crystal glasses, and flowers. It was festive and engaging for good eating.

At work I developed a very nice growing clientele. One day, Robert's client asked me if I heard about a session taking place in the building about hypnotism. I was curious, studying supernatural powers, the stars, etc. So I went. There was a room full of people standing and one speaker talking about power. He used his tricks, and suddenly everybody went down, like flies. I was the only one standing. He looked at me and said, "Your will is overpowering mine." He was in disbelief. I was kind of surprised.

Laurent was with us most of the weekends, and he liked the new arrangement. He enjoyed the picnics, playing ball, petanque. One weekend, without Laurent — he was with his father — Robert decided to put me behind the wheel of his car. I was excited to take my first driving lesson. It was impressive to control such a big machine. I really liked it, so I would practice, but only on the weekends in a small town. We had a wonderful life, work was great, my son was in a safe place, and our little apartment was lovely. We had gourmet meals, no fights, no arguments, a smooth loving time.

One day I got a phone call from Mrs. Parizy; she was very upset. She had waited few days to tell me about it. She was on her balcony, on the tenth floor, watching for Laurent to come home from school, when an unknown man began talking to him. She realized something was wrong, but by the time she came down, he had disappeared. She was frantic. Where was the child! She went toward the park and started knocking on people's doors. She got no response. She frantically looked for Laurent. Suddenly, the unknown man brought my son to her. She was so thankful and relieved.

On the way back to the apartment, she asked him questions. Laurent said the man urinated on him, put his hand on his mouth, and told him to be quiet. Mrs. Parizy gave him a bath and changed his clothes. She was too upset to tell me. She even got shingles from the ordeal — from the stress. After the news, I went to school to inform them about the incident, to warn them about child predators. They had noticed him around the grounds but didn't think it was suspicious. I don't think Laurent had any recollections.

We were approached by a salon owner, Felix, from Salon Galatee. He offered us a good deal, so the three of us — Robert, Bettina, and I — moved to Rue Lecourbe, a small shop that gave the feeling of being in a living room, very personal. We liked the owners also, a middle-aged couple with a white poodle. They lived not far from where we worked. Felix's wife rarely came. We brought with us a large, faithful clientele; we were known in the neighborhood as stylish and smart. Yvette followed me as well as her sisters. Since I got my place on Rue Platon, I didn't go anymore to the Madeleine's for lunch. Sometimes I would buy some clothes and say hello. I was still close to the family and would remain their friends for the rest of my life. Rue Lecourbe, like Rue Levis, became a marketplace every morning of the week except Sundays. Merchants came, built their stands, and sold their goods, fresh picked early morning. The street had many shops from charcuteries, fish markets, liquor stores, fresh produce, butchers, bakeries, cosmetics, designers, cleaners . . . everything was available. Bettina's apartment was on that street, a little further from the market. Only the stretch where Salon Galatee was located had all the business and the buzzing. We loved it! Robert and Bettina shopped for food there all the time. I remembered trying sea urchin, a shell delicatessen. It was so fine, so sweet. Across from the shop, tucked behind two stores, was Jean's business. I had to push a heavy wooden door to enter a courtyard. On the right there were steps to get to his place, a shack. He was making preserved kumquats. He used huge copper bowls to marinate the exotic fruits for a whole day. It was fascinating. He would sell them to Chinese restaurants or present them in gift boxes to bakeries or pastry shops. It was a lucrative business. Colette, his wife, owned a small skin care spa two doors down from him. She was beautiful with very blue eyes and dark blond hair. Jean was heavy with big blue eyes, always smiling, and a big heart when he liked the person. He was a great businessman. One day he told us his story.

Jean had joined the Green Berets and went to Kenya. While there, the natives elected him the "wise man," the judge. They sat him under the biggest tree in a huge chair made out of sugar cane to judge and advise the citizens. He relished these stories and when we would get together we would hear about his life in Africa, always entertaining. I knew he was more than a friend. He would do anything for me and go out of his way to help me. We had a bond without words, and I admired and respected him. I loved his wife and daughter. I felt great among them, protected and loved.

I met another special person, Odette. She lived in the same building where we worked. She came to me to have her hair done, always tired. Her mother, Valentine, getting instructions for chores to be done. Odette was a short, small lady, eighteen years my elder, energetic, witty, smart, good sense of humor, and always on the go. I learned she had a business selling vegetables and fruits. She had a booth at the Halles, which was world famous for the wholesale produce market. She would buy directly from the producers, displaying the merchandise in her booth and pricing it like the stock market, high first then lower to get rid of it. You really have to know what you are doing, act fast, move constantly, and be friendly. It's a person-to-person business. If they like you, they come to you first; you have to get rid of your goods. Some fruits and vegetables came from all over the world, even Israel and South America. She had to sell what she had, so she was at work at four o'clock in the morning whether there was rain, snow, cold, or heat. The middle man would come, bargain, buy, and toward the end it would be auctioned. You had to be fast, know your mathematics, and take a chance. I wanted to see the process so one day I went with her. I was amazed! I learned a lot. These people deserved a lot of credit. In the winter it was freezing — no heaters — and you had to move, to be on top of everything. I developed a great friendship and admiration for Odette. By watching her in action, it gave me the desire to own a business one day. Her companion, Zacca, was a competitor, and after becoming close they merged. They became the biggest wholesaler of fruits and vegetables. They went around the world, by boat, twice! They were happy and successful, buying an estate in Morsang sur Seine. It had a lot of land, a pond, a windmill, a waterfront with a pier to dock the boats, an impressive perimeter of poplars, and a long driveway leading up to a wrought iron gate. An amazing show place. On the property, there was a small house with double doors opening to the living room, a huge kitchen with double windows opening toward the woods, a bathroom with a round window, and a staircase leading to the bedrooms — with exposed beams and roof. In front of the kitchen and the living room was a patio with big cement pots, a white gazebo shading the sun, and beautiful flowers all around. I spent many weekends there. But like many things, some people are never content. Zacca left her for his secretary. She never got over it.

Robert and I were doing well. We looked for an apartment and found one outside Paris toward the south, in a town called Chilly Mazarin. Our apartment was on the third floor with two bedrooms, big windows, and a balcony. I made our nest cozy. Robert was very handy. He dressed the entrance with a pleated, red ruby-paisley cloth from the crystal chandelier on an angle to the wall and then down to the wooden floor where I put a Persian rug. It fell like being under a Pasha's tent. We had a big bathroom, living room, dining room, and a great kitchen. In Europe, the kitchen was just a room with a sink. You had to furnish it with appliances, as well as the lighting. I finally started to breathe, to come out of my hole.

On Sunday morning, there was an open market, like at home. We would go and browse. I met a man there and we started talking. He told me I looked like one of the ladies on the canvas he was painting. I became interested. He invited me to come to his studio. I was impressed by his magnitude of work, the diversity, the bright colors, their luminosity. I bought four of them and proudly hung them on our walls. Bettina came to spend the weekend with us. We became very close. We were so similar though physically opposite. She was petite, tan, dark hair, Asian looking, exotic. I was very white, thin, and petite. We had the same taste, and our priorities were also similar. We had both gone through divorces; the only difference was that I had Laurent.

Our life was idealistic, for the time being. We had gourmet meals and lived in luxury compared to our peers.

We went skiing, camping, and were even invited to go hunting in the region of Sologne, at our boss's relative's house. That weekend I didn't have Laurent.

Very early on a Sunday morning, I tucked my white pants in my boots, my white top opened, and had on my beige jacket with zippers everywhere. Robert was also well put together. He got his shotgun, and away we went. Living in the south, we took the interstate via Orleans, which was in the Sologne. We enjoyed the beautiful country and many amazing estates along the way. As we drove to the entrance, we stopped at a huge iron gate with a guard. We gave our names and the gate opened. We traveled quite some time, and on each side of us there were flowers, manicured ornamental trees, and then fields. At the end of the road, there was the castle, so impressive with its columns, steps, and big double doors. We parked the car in the designated spot and the owner greeted us and introduced us to other guests. Felix was a far back relative of the owner. The land was used for hunting for a fee to take care of the place, the animals, and the birds. The game warden orchestrated the hunt. People were well screened. The group all got acquainted. We went to a designated field, starting with the birds that were kept under a net and then freed. Then the pheasants, ducks, and rabbits were all released. We were put on a straight line, alternating guns and observers, so the hunters were spread to prevent accidents. The warden himself had lost an eye during a hunt, so the rules were strictly observed. The land was immense, so we went by Jeep. The field had high grass, and the quails flew over us. *Boom!* One shot, one down, and so on. It was a very interesting day. The hunting dogs were alert, loving the game, proud to be part of it. The sky was a deep blue, like you see in the country, no

pollution, and it was warm with a little breeze. At the end of
the hunt, we put all our prey under the porch of the castle,
and the warden would give each hunter one game of each
selection. Then we were invited for a late lunch.

As we entered, there was the hall where we gave our
jackets and purses to a gentleman, and then we went to the
dining room. It had a high ceiling with a big chandelier
made of deer antlers interlaced with lights, a huge fireplace
you could sit in front of on cement benches, big paintings
with hunting themes, and a very long table dressed with
elegance. I had never seen a table like this. In the middle
were three flower arrangements mixed with branches of
nuts, acorns, and a candelabra with lit candles. The table
setting had different sizes of plates put on a pewter server
with hunting scenes. The flatware was made out of antlers,
and the beverages were poured into goblets made out
of horns. It was very grand and a reminder of the hunt.
We had waiters all dressed, serving us, checking for any
of our desires. The menu included pate of wild boar and
garlicky, parsley frog legs. The waiters came with a bowl of
water with a slice of lemon to rinse our fingers. The main
course was a barbecued doe basted with juices and herbs
and served with mushrooms, vegetables, and small fried
potatoes, then a green salad and an assortment of cheeses.
We tasted different wines during the meal. After dinner, we
went to a different room for coffee and dessert. That room
was also breathtaking with another big fireplace, antiques,
paintings, fancy lighting, rugs, and tapestries hanging on
the walls. We mingled with the guests before it was time
to depart with our trophies. We thanked our host and left.
Felix came with us. We had reservations in a hotel in the
next town. We had a very busy day, and we were not used to

all that fresh air and walking on rough ground. We slept well that night, happy.

On our way back, we exchanged our thoughts and recollections of the day. Felix told us the remainder of the game was delivered to a hospital. It made us happy that it wasn't going to waste. Back home, Bettina and Robert put a tasty dinner on the table of basted pheasant and flambé with a cognac sauce.

Robert loved ballet so we decided to see Rudolph Nuryev and his partner Galina Ulanova. The critics couldn't stop raving about them. The performance was in an amphitheater built on the belt around Paris. Every seat had a great view. The ballet was impressive, unlike any I had ever seen. So much power and grace. We were glued to the stage, no one was moving, our eyes following the dancers, their jumps, their pas de deux, Nuryev's expressions. He was an unbelievable animal with his muscles, his moves, his high jumps. She was so graceful, bending so low and then back up so gracefully, unbreakable, fragile. The show was unforgettable.

Robert finally separated from his wife and daughter. He rarely spoke about it. My parents wanted to meet the man I was living with, so we decided to drive to Cernay, Alsace, with Laurent. We left at four o'clock in the morning so there would be no traffic. We stopped for an earthy breakfast and to relax. My parents hadn't seen Laurent for some time! I wasn't worried; Robert was easy going. He was the eldest of five, and his mother handled the family with grace and humor. My parents were very happy to see us, and they welcomed Robert. We brought with us a box of Marron Glace (glazed chestnuts), my mother's favorite. It put a smile on her face. My father took the reins and led Robert on a

tour to see his friends and play billiards, while Mother and
I caught up with my latest move. Mother had prepared one
of my favorite meals. We all gathered around a festive table.
Father opened some of his best wines to celebrate our visit.
Then we went to see my sister and her husband, then my
brother and his wife and daughter, Cornelia. We felt very
welcomed. Time goes by fast when you have a good trip,
seeing family, reconnecting. We had a great weekend, and it
made the coming week happier at work.

By now we would have lunch at Jean's place every day we
worked. Robert would cook, I would set the table with odd
plates, and Bettina, Jean, Robert, and I would sit around it
and had fun. These were happy times. Bettina and Roland
were in love. His parents wanted to meet us, so they invited
us for lunch one Sunday. They came to Paris from North
Africa when the French left their country. They had a hard
time providing for their family, so they decided to immigrate
to America (Florida), where the father had a brother. They
were very sweet and loving.

We worked together as a team, and our clientele was
growing. We were well-known and made a lot of money.
Bettina got a fennec fox for company. Her mother wanted
to meet me, so we were invited for lunch. With a bouquet
of flowers in my hands, I met her mother, who received
us with open arms. To my recollection, she had black hair,
black almond-shaped eyes, and warm like her daughter. We
also met Bettina's brother who was puzzled by our looks and
openness. Now I knew why Bettina was such a good cook;
her mother's meal was superb.

Robert's parents also wanted to see us, so we took the
road toward Lyon. The scenery was beautiful; I always
enjoyed nature. They lived in an apartment with the twins,

Alain and Williams. They were all glad to see us. Robert's father was subdued, laid back, studying me. His mother was loving, and we connected instantly. His twin brothers were young and fun. Williams devoured me with his eyes. He was very good looking with unusual, big green eyes. He reminded me of James Dean with the same stoned, cool look, covering an accumulation of strong feelings, rebellion. He was distant but I knew I made a big impression on him. Robert's mother was open, friendly, and coquettish. She was of Greek descent and proud of her children, protective. I didn't have any rapport or conversation with his father. He was almost nonexistent. The household was very noisy, full of life. It was different from anything I had experienced. I was eager to introduce Robert to Mittelwhir, a place that brought me a lot of happiness, a place very close to my heart, to show him the evolution of wine making and the unbelievable spectacle of the vineyards on rolling hills basting in the sun.

By now, Grandmama had a two-story house in rough-cast cement on the foot of some vineyard. Aunt Amelie and Uncle Eric ran the household. They had added vineyards to their estate — the start of developing a grand industry. They had two children, one son, Philippe, to whom I am the godmother, and a daughter, Nicole. They exported wine to America. We tasted wine, had some cold cuts famous from the region, and sat around a friendly table, laughing, recalling our vacation at the barrack. Before we left, Uncle Eric gave us a bottle of his wine as a present; we were very appreciative.

We went back to Paris, bringing great memories, and shared them with Bettina. We went to the movies to see *Ben Hur*. A lady from the crowd came up to me and said, "You are going to America." I was stunned, then laughed and forgot about it.

People weren't happy. There was a lot of unemployment and strikes everywhere, every week. It became difficult to get around, to work, because the traffic was unbelievable; we all were frustrated. We were sitting around idle when Jean, a coworker, told us he was approached by somebody he knew to take a job in Washington DC, America. I was excited for him, but he wasn't. Jean was in the middle of a bitter divorce and couldn't leave the country. He gave us the information and connections. Robert and I saw the opportunity to have something one day, a business and a home, which was impossible here. We decided Robert had to go first. I had to take care of Laurent and see how things went; it would change the direction of our lives. I put Robert on the plane and away he went to America!

I never realized the impact of his absence, how comfortable it was to be with someone. I readjusted my life. Working saved me. Robert's clients flocked to me, so I stayed busy. Living in Chilly Mazarin was too far, too lonely. Mrs. Parizy found a studio for rent in her building on the first floor. I moved. So now I had Laurent every night; my little boy gave me such comfort. Robert wrote me often, telling me about his new ventures in America. He made a friend, Jacques, a French man from the Basque region, south of France, close to the Pyrenees. He took Robert under his wings. Jacques worked for Elisabeth Arden and Robert for Jean-Paul. Jacques was established, and Robert knew the latest styles and techniques. His looks, his engagement, and his gregarious style were more than welcome by the manager and the clients. He rented a one bedroom in the same building as his new friend. I really started to miss Robert a lot. But as least I had my friends. They invited me out often.

Bettina met her future husband, Claude. I liked him on the spot. I loved seeing her so happy and content; it was a positive sign for a long life together. They started living under the same roof. He was a reporter. I thought he was interesting, different from anybody she had ever met. They complemented each other. One evening, while having dinner together, I told Bettina my plans for my future. I was definitely going to America. Between the socialist government tying my hands and having no assets, meaning no loans, I had no future here. I had great ideas. Maybe I was over my head, but I was never afraid to work hard, to stand on my feet, to use my skills and education. She knew me so well, understood me, and agreed. It was the only way for me to get a better life and keep my child. My ex-husband, Jacques, was becoming increasingly interested in his son; it kind of warned me of what was coming. Laurent was the first grandchild born in a Jewish family, who carried their name. I had a strong feeling things were not going to be smooth.

My brother, Francis, came to live with me. Father was very domineering and wanted his son to be exposed to a high-class clientele, to improve his work as a hair stylist. Francis didn't enjoy what he was doing. We got along, and I finally got connected with him. He loved to cook; what a blessing! He was very nice to Laurent, and we learned about each other. He loved me, admired me. After few months, Father called him to come home. He didn't want to lose his son to the big city. Back home, Francis didn't like working under Father's control, so he ended up leaving the profession. He got a job in Basel, Switzerland, working for Roche, the pharmaceutical company. He loved it. He was his own boss within the company. He later became manager in his section.

My sister, Annick, married a young man of German descent. We were the same age. He always wanted to be with me, and I couldn't stand him. He was arrogant, narcissistic, a know-it-all. Around him I stayed low key; I knew something was going to happen one day. My sister opened her own salon and put her daughter to work with her, as my father did.

Meanwhile, the correspondence between Robert and I became sparse. I called often. I had to stay in touch and make important decisions. I spoke to my parents to see if they would take care of Laurent while I settled in America, so he wouldn't be too disturbed by the enormous changes. I took some classes in English at Berlitz, so I could at least say few words. I said good-bye to Mrs. Parizy. She was very sad. She was attached to Laurent and considered him like a son; he had lived with her for so long. But she understood my situation. My ex-husband seldom paid her. I had to change my budget and seldom took Laurent on designated weekends. She knew the struggle and suspected my ex-husband, Jacques, would attempt to take Laurent away from me in the near future. We hugged and cried. I took the train to Mulhouse, with my son, to the school to enroll him. For everybody it was a big commitment, a change of lifestyle. By this time, Mother was fifty-eight, and Father was fifty-four. My father encouraged me, though he was skeptical for me to go to a capitalist country. He never voiced his feelings; he just accepted my decisions and backed me up. Before I left I wanted to go the mountains where we went so often. I truly loved that place. Father complied. It was a touristy place with many buses from all over. We walked a narrow trail to get to a scenic spot; it was breathtaking. There were rolling hills covered with white crosses for American soldiers who died there saving us, giving us our liberty back. The tunnels are still there. You enter on one side and exit on the other. It gave me a sense of respect, dignity for the loss of life. There was also an unknown tomb for the slaughtered, unidentified. Very somber. My thoughts tried to recapture the scene. The thoughts of these brave men, their dedication, it was overwhelming. I felt humbled. Now I was going to their country. I took the train back. I gave a big hug to Laurent and told him to be a good boy. Father and Mother held me very tightly with tears streaming. Laurent didn't understand what was going on. My parents had never showed me any feelings. This was the first time, and I was touched. I gave up my apartment, and Odette took me in the last month. I moved some of my stuff: some to my parents' house and some stuff I gave to my colleagues. I sent a few things overseas.

Life at Odette's was the best. Her apartment in Paris was small, comfortable, and inviting. On Saturday, after work, we drove to Morsang sur Seine. A high-cemented wall surrounded the property with a pond full of fish and a windmill, which was transformed into a guest quarters. A pier, from where we jumped into the river, was across from a restaurant that was very busy on weekends. It was a very busy river with lots of boats, sailboats, motorboats, yachts, and long commercial barges. There was also a sad side. We saw a young, homeless man named Yvon. Odette helped him by giving him some tasks to do at the Halles and gave him a room in a small house on the property. He was depressed and never spoke to anybody. I tried to be friendly and help, but he didn't let me. Before long, a boater found his body down the river under a bridge. I was devastated. The town was very picturesque with small, hilly streets and houses built tightly together with high walls for privacy. Many Americans and high-level government people had their second homes there.

Odette's house was a doll house. I loved it. We had breakfast outside under a huge white gazebo where we would watch the boats and the ducks; it was very relaxing. Back to Paris we battled the heavy traffic, but we were glad to be home. I heard about a lady telling the future, who lived not far from the shop. I made an appointment to see her. I could feel my relationship with Robert was vanishing. The distance, the letters becoming rarer . . . I just wanted to be reassured, so I went.

She was attractive. She looked at me with intensity, yet a soft smile lit up her face. She said, "You are going to America. You are going to be successful. You will meet a man, thirty-six years old, never married, a European. You are going to live a long time but will have some health issues." Leaving her apartment I felt better, but there were still a lot of unknowns.

There was an uprising in Paris, people were unhappy, the minimum wage was too low, and the students were revolting. Ruby the Rogue started to stir up the people, paralyzing France completely. The universities, as well as the factories were occupied by anarchists and the unions were paralyzing the economy. He became famous for a short time. It was impossible to go to work because everybody was on strike, except me. They even locked down my apartment. I had to jump out of a window and walk to the shop. The students went to the streets and destroyed businesses, breaking their windows with the cobble stones from the streets. At that time I had no political affiliation. I still had a picture of Che Guevara in my studio. Seeing this destruction of my beautiful Paris, my point of view changed. These students were lucky to have wealthy parents who could afford to send them to these expensive schools. The police picked me up, put me in their car, drove me to the nearest police station amid my protests, and then released me for lack of evidence. I took the metro and went back to my secure world. I was restless. To witness such violence was beyond me. I started to dislike the unions. I had to walk two hours to get to work, and every week there was another strike. My thoughts swirled in my head. *What am I going to achieve in my life?* I was raised to be a fighter, to reach goals, starting from the bottom up. I admired pioneers in the new world: Alexander Fleming for discovering penicillin, Thomas Edison for discovering the light bulb. This was the way to go ahead, not by destruction. I wanted to make our lives more enjoyable, to live with quality and beauty. *So where do I fit in?*

The opportunity knocked at my door, and I listened without hesitation. I took the offer. AMERICA. The promised land, where everything was possible with hard work. I was ready.

At Odette's country place, we had our last gathering for my farewell to America. I met a man from a Middle Eastern Arabic region, a very interesting individual, who asked me why I was leaving Paris, France, such a beautiful country. I explained my goals. He understood and proposed to discover Paris by night. I accepted. He picked me up at seven o'clock in the evening in a DS, the latest Citroen sports car, loaded with accessories. It was a beauty. I was excited to discover an unknown side of my beloved city. We had dinner at a restaurant in Saint Cloud, very grand, elegant, then hopped from one nightclub to another. He knew I loved to dance, so I did, all night, by myself, taking the dance floor like a ballerina. I always wanted to be one. I was in my own world. People watched and applauded, asking for more. My companion just enjoyed the show. The sun started to show its golden striking rim, giving the sky a vibrant glow, the end of a memorable night, the beginning of the last morning in Paris for some years to come. I thanked my chauffeur, and he walked me to the door where we said good-bye. I turned another page.

A few hours later, I was in my designated seat, flying above Paris, leaving behind my beloved son, my family, my friends, everything I always knew. My stomach cramped with anxiety overwhelming my soul and mind. This was my first time flying. Having danced all night I shriveled in my seat, closed my eyes, a pillow under my head covered with a blanket, exhausted. I thought of what would be awaiting me on my grand leap over the ocean.

FROM PARIS to WASHINGTON

CPSIA information can be obtained
at www.ICGtesting.com
Printed in the USA
BVHW041700120419
545373BV00008B/63/P